MILK DRUNK

MILK DRUNK

DRUNK

what to expect when you're not expecting

DANIELLE SCHWARTZ

Milk Drunk: What to Expect When You Are Not Expecting

© 2024 by Danielle Schwartz

Library of Congress Control Number: 2024911715
ISBN: 978-1-954676-98-5 (paperback)   978-1-954676-99-2 (ebook)

This book is based on true events reflecting the author's memory of them. Some names and characteristics may have been changed, some events compressed, and some dialogue recreated.

Editors: Deborah Froese, Madelyn Elizabeth Sipola, Dianna Graveman
Cover and Interior Design: Emma Elzinga

Printed in the United States of America

First Edition

3 West Garden Street, Ste. 718
Pensacola, FL 32502
www.indigoriverpublishing.com

Ordering Information:

Quantity sales: Special discounts are available on quantity purchases by corporations, associations, and others. For details, contact the publisher at the address above.

Orders by US trade bookstores and wholesalers: Please contact the publisher at the address above.

With Indigo River Publishing, you can always expect great books, strong voices, and meaningful messages. Most importantly, you'll always find . . . *words worth reading.*

CONTENTS

INTRODUCTION

Have you ever doubted or constantly defended yourself to others because the decisions you made were different from theirs?

Of course you have!

Society triggers conformity, and who doesn't want to belong, right? Wrong.

I *definitely* have experience from the "outsiders'" perspective, and it all stems from my decision to not have children. From defending myself to friends, acquaintances, coworkers, and even strangers who don't agree with *my* decision, to getting berated for being a "horrible" person because my sole purpose as a woman is to "make babies," I have heard it all and have always remained content in my decision, which is why I chose to write this book.

Now, before you decide if you want to board the Hot Mess Express, let me explain what this book is *not* about.

1. There will be no lectures, debates, or lengthy details expressing my opinion about whether someone should have a child. If you are looking for someone or something to provide guidance during your internal child limbo debate, then I suggest you put this book down and look within your heart.

2. This book is not an outlet for bashing parents or children. I'm simply sharing my personal experiences with people and their reactions to my non-baby mama journey.

3. Lastly, while some of the experiences I discuss involve sensitive topics, I am in no way attacking these beliefs, situations, or ways of life.

OK, now that we got that business out of the way, let's chitchat about what you *will* read in this adventure.

This book details my memorable encounters and conversations involving my decision not to have children. Some people truly commend the courage, self-awareness, and determination an uncommon choice like this takes, while others believe I have let God, my family, my femininity, and even the world down. Imagine being told you've let down the whole world? Talk about some serious stress! Especially when you didn't realize the whole world was looking at you.

Since the world is looking, and there is seemingly a growing population of child-free people, my book on what to expect when you are not expecting provides reasons to communicate this taboo and socially unaccustomed story.

Before we get too far ahead and the haters come out and say I am anti-baby and anti-motherhood, let me emphasize that it is the farthest thing from the truth. I do love children, and I completely understand that parents are strong and amazing superheroes. With that being said, I am simply taking this opportunity to discuss my child-free journey, highlighting all the questions, conversations, and even "hatorade" that has flowed in my direction. Knowing there are many childless people like me out there, I hope my voice provides an outlet and comfort for this community while providing others "ah-ha" moments and a view to this particular life perspective.

With all that out of the way, let me formally introduce myself.

I am a fierce, forty-something, independent woman working as a senior manager of product development in a substantial career. I have a loving husband named Jim, who is my best friend, a great family, and a fulfilling life.

What I don't have is a child. By choice.

I grew up in New Jersey, circa 1979. In all actuality, I should be used to judgments, being from the Garden State, which has a reputation as the *armpit of America*; however, it's a state that offers more than oil refineries and drunken, classless out-of-towners (sorry, Snooki). Instead, it is a state that offers city life, diversity, and picturesque atmospheres. On any given day, one can go apple picking, swim at some incredible shores, hop on a train and be in New York City in less than twenty minutes, or snowboard at multiple ski locations.

Growing up in this environment offered me authentic growth, strong family values, unconditional love, and amazing traditions that proved to be the necessary ingredients for my recipe of life. From an early age, family bonds were the key driver for my motivation and morals. Even though not one sibling, cousin, aunt, or uncle from my large, diverse family has the same personality, we all seem to speak the same language. My family's love, loyalty, and values allow me to feel comfortable exploring everything life has to offer, which includes a life without a child. They welcome my savage personality, but more importantly, they support my desire to try new opportunities.

With an adventurous and curious nature, I love to travel and explore different cultures. When I'm not exploring, you can find me excitedly inventing dessert recipes, enthusiastically airplane spotting, embracing thrill-seeking activities, visiting sporting arenas, or growing my science knowledge. Even at an early age, these passions were constant ambitions in my life to try something new, which had a significant influence on my decision not to have children.

I was sixteen years old when I realized I did not want to have children. I know some people may think that's a young age for a life-changing realization, but I tapped deep inside to understand myself and what made me happy. Was having a child a lifetime opportunity that I could not let pass by? Or would it prevent me from experiencing a life I felt was passing *me* by?

From the very beginning, I knew child-rearing came with constant variables that could prevent new opportunities I was or would be willing to take.

And no, I didn't have all those answers at sixteen, but I knew I had the right to choose for myself. A life with a child was not the choice for me. I wasn't destined to be a mom. No biological clock ticked, and there was no fear my life would not be fulfilled. Instead, I chose to focus on what was important to me and which destination I'd go to next.

So grab your tickets, because the Hot Mess Express is pulling out of the station.

Chapter 1
PURPOSE

"What is the purpose of your life if you aren't a mother?"

L et's play a game.

Consider specific words people use to describe you. As you mentally scroll through the list, think about the most common statements—those frequently used remarks that portray your personality in one neatly tied bow. Are the majority of the descriptions correct, or do you feel the world views you from the surface?

My own library of perceptions ranges from independent and considerate to the blatantly obvious child-free, which is a decision I've been explaining almost my whole life.

So, the question, "What's your purpose in life if you're not going to have a baby?" is one that follows me around like a lost puppy.

Sigh.

Throughout history, a woman's economic value has focused on her capacity to bear children, despite the many successful and life-changing women in the world. Take for example Judith Heumann, a long-time disability rights advocate who protested for the passage of the Rehabilitation Act, advised Presidents Clinton and Obama, and pushed for the globalization of disability rights. Or Katherine Johnson, the mathematical genius whose computations successfully launched astronaut John Glenn into orbit in 1962 and sent Apollo 11 to the moon.[1]

What gives, people?

From ancient times, it has been customary to define a woman as limited and contingent compared to a man. Typical definitions from societal pressures confine a woman to positions of dependency with the value focused on their capacity for pregnancy.[2] Even in today's advanced age, culture, economy, family upbringing, and geography, these still play a pivotal role.

The recession evident in today's economy suggests people are choosing to have fewer children.[3] Inconsistent income, currency value, and cost of living play a much larger role with life decisions. For example, when a twelve pack of my favorite soda costs three dollars more, the contemplation of worth sets in, and an internal debate occurs in aisle nine.

All that over Diet Mountain Dew.

Deciding to purchase this delicious, carbonated treat is not a major life decision, just one that took consideration based on the economy. If I took ten minutes in Stop and Shop to determine my future beverage of choice, imagine the effort and thought needed for something more substantial . . . like a baby?

The US Census indicates a steady decline in births from 2019, pre-pandemic, to December 2021, current pandemic, with an average decline of 4.06 percent in 2020 alone.[4] Living within a worldwide pandemic, employment instability, and the inner drive for

1   Cassie Hurwitz, "38 Inspiring Women Who Changed the World," *Oprah Daily*, Feb. 10, 2023, https://www.oprahdaily.com/life/g26513857/women-who-changed-the-world/.

2   Marilyn Boxer, "Women, Historical and Cross-Cultural Perspectives," Encyclopedia.com, 1995, http://www.encyclopedia.com/science/encyclopedias-almanacs-transcripts-maps/women-historical-and-cross-cultural-perspectives.

3   Anne Morse, "U.S Births Declined During the Pandemic," United States Census Bureau, September 21, 2021, http://www.census.gov/library/stories/2021/09/united-states-births-declined-during-the-pandemic.html.

4   Ibid.

self-discovery, people are choosing to focus on their personal cycle versus their fertility cycle.

Early on, discussing my child-free decisions with new acquaintances had me drowning in confused thoughts, emotions, and guilt. Despite my confidence, the consistent barrage of questions, concerns, and even verbal abuse became overwhelming—almost to the point where I considered altering my view.

Almost.

Conversations about my decision were not going away, so I had to find a way to respond without letting fear intimidate me. As I learned to do that, I felt more buoyant, and the negative emotions became positive affirmations. The floaties came off, and I was ready to do laps in the giant pool we call society!

When I was in my late twenties, I attended a birthday party for my friend's ten-year-old daughter. The outdoor playground was filled with colorful decorations, enough pizza to feed a small town, parents happily relaxing, adult juice boxes, and an abundance of children enjoying life. I mingled between groups and played with the kids throughout the day. During a moment sitting alone at a table, an older woman—probably in her sixties—approached me with a sweet expression and inquisitive nature.

"Which one of these children is yours?" she asked.

With sincere eyes, I shook my head and said, "None."

"Oh." She stared directly at me. "Do you have a family?"

With a smile I answered, "Yes, a husband and a very large, tight-knit family."

Afraid she might assume I was at the children's party for obscure reasons, I felt inclined to quickly defend my attendance.

"I'm here for my friend's daughter's birthday," I swiftly stated.

After my statement, I felt her level of sincerity and observation. Those genuine attributes, along with her relaxed frame and honest smile, helped me feel comfortable. Without hesitation, she seamlessly pointed out with pride her blonde-haired granddaughter.

After that, we struck up a warm conversation around family. She spoke about her four children, how one had died of leukemia, and the insufferable pain she encountered from that loss.

While discussing her child's death, she happily stared at the children playing.

Slowly, she turned to me, "Even though I buried my child, I wouldn't change my life. My purpose is to be a mother no matter what the circumstances are."

I sat there humbled and hooked on every word. The emotion in her eyes wasn't just sorrow, but honor, and I wanted to experience more.

Thankfully, she continued the conversation.

"What is your purpose then, dear?" she politely asked.

I placed my hand on my chest. "To be the best version of me."

She sweetly smiled, and we sat there in a friendly silence watching the children play.

In a world where curiosity is at the helm with obstacles preventing an easy or straightforward journey, assumption is its neighbor.

As a female you will constantly get asked if you have children, with the assumption you want kids. Case in point, the older woman at the birthday party. Though harmless, her icebreaker was wildly incorrect. In her defense, the odds were high that someone my age was attending the party because their child was invited; however, these assumptions happen with or without Bozo the Clown entertaining.

If you've made the decision to remain child-free—whether it be the timing, medical issues, or grief from losing a child—it is good to start preparing answers now. The moment you state, "I don't have children," you'll face an awkward pause as the person questioning you determines why and how *they* will react.

Trust me, reactions vary.

Is it because you can't have children? That reasoning garners an empathetic response accompanied by a head tilt, a gentle touch on your arm for support, and a slow closing of the eyes to reassure you everything will be OK.

Is it because you are young and want to wait? That reasoning receives an encouraging response, followed with the spontaneous laugh and a dismissive hand wave emphasizing time is on your side.

Is it because you chose not to have children? That response can go in multiple directions. You might get a gentle touch on the arm showing pride or a maniacal laugh indicating you'll change your mind. You might also get the angry confrontation, the inquisitive conversationalist, the supportive hug, or even the lost soul looking for answers. With any direction, remember to listen and answer however *you* choose, remaining true to yourself.

Becoming our best selves is difficult. Constantly striving to remain true to yourself will undoubtedly stir challenges affecting your journey. Stress, disappointment, depression, and criticality are common denominators, according to psychologists and philosophers.

Psychologist Stephen Joseph emphasizes, "Living inauthentically, when what we say and do does not match how we think and feel, creates an inner psychological tension that can be distressing. If we live inauthentically, day after day, it is likely to take an emotional toll on us."[5] Each person has the responsibility to create life paths based on uniqueness and potential. By ignoring those responsibilities, a step further from authenticity occurs.

Because these struggles are real, people might not immediately recognize their own special potential. Instead, they could find themselves settling for what others want or expect. For example, research conducted by Bronnie Ware, an Australian palliative nurse, concluded the most common regret of those on their deathbed was lacking the courage to live a life true to themselves.[6]

Imagine living a life that at the end you realized wasn't yours?

That is no life at all.

In situations where you find yourself teeter-tottering between your

---

5   Stephen Joseph, *Authentic: How to Be Yourself and Why It Matters* (London: Piatkus, 2016).

6   Joseph, *Authentic: How to Be Yourself and Why It Matters.*

real self and anything else, simply remember what Dr. Seuss (Theodore Geisel) is reported to have once said: "Be who you are and say what you feel because those who mind don't matter and those who matter don't mind."

My purpose in life does not involve being a mother, and that is OK. I fully support motherhood for others, just not for me. I do plan my life in accordance with well-natured virtues: being the best wife, sister, daughter, friend, and human being I can be, which involves deep roots of integrity, humility, curiosity, nurturing, and charity. Remaining true to myself and living happily as I can is key, because at any moment of this temporary existence, my defined purpose can shift.

The question, "What defines you?" is so subjective, so broad, and yet so personal. The world consistently demonstrates two attributes that support defining us: our patience when we have nothing and our attitude when we have everything. These tests spotlight our attitudes and set boundaries within. If you have everything you've ever wanted, how do you treat others? Are you sincere and humble, or cold and selfish? If you have little in life, how do you view it? Are you thankful for what you have, or do you blame the world for your problems? No situations or attitudes are this binary; however, these examples show scenarios that force us to look within, react, and accept layers defining us.

Being defined is all about the layers. To be defined as one thing is kind of vanilla—conventional and basic. Not that vanilla is bad; it is my favorite ice cream flavor. I just can't see myself eating plain vanilla ice cream for the rest of my life. Personally, I'm more vanilla with a ton of rainbow sprinkles on a cone that is placed in a dish.

My husband would say, "High maintenance but thinks she's low maintenance!"

I can't deny that statement.

High maintenance because my desires are complicated and tailored. Yes, I want vanilla ice cream in a sugar cone. Since I eat slowly, I want that cone in a cup. I also want the rainbow sprinkles and not the chocolate ones (to me there is a difference in taste and texture). Fully aware that my wants can be difficult, I understand the possibility they won't be met, which brings in my low-maintenance side.

I take pride in articulating my defined layers: An independent woman aware of who she is and what she wants. A caring individual who has strong morals, work ethic, compassion, and loyalty. A pessimist who believes in science and is not afraid to take risks. I challenge myself to learn and grow, and I firmly believe that life only has one guarantee—a beginning and an end.

See? Lots of rainbow sprinkles.

Having a meaningful discussion with yourself identifies needs but also your wants out of life. I am not talking about mundane, everyday discussions around what you'll have for dinner; instead I am talking about something deeper—like brunch. Just kidding! These conversations are establishing your identity and allowing yourself to define reality. Do I work in the family business because it is expected of me, or should I pursue my dream of becoming an actor even though my family believes it's not a respectable career? Can I make my community proud even if I come out as gay, or should I stay living a lie to protect the neighborhood? How can I make a positive change in the world if I am conflicted about my courage to evoke change? These questions are examples of deep internal discussions that can pave the wants, needs, and identities of life.

Truth be told, everyone will judge your purpose, even if it imitates theirs. So why not set it to your own standards, which could affect the most positive outcome?

To have a purpose in life, you need to find yourself, and to do that you need to think for yourself. Thinking for yourself does not mean shutting everyone out and only caring for you. Instead, this approach confirms your identity as an individual, shows what is needed for growth, and instills the confidence to ask for it.

As the youngest in my family, the stigma that I needed to be coddled, spoke for, and managed was dominant. This was no fault of my family's, as I was not planned and a surprise in an environment that was settled; however, that stigma carried well over its prime. In order for me to believe my capabilities, I knew I had to step out of their shadows and demonstrate being an adult. I maintained the same job from sixteen years old until after college graduation when I was twenty-three. I know this dedication began my well-rounded work ethic.

I went to college at West Virginia University, which was far away from my family in New Jersey. I knew the leap from my family's safety net would be difficult, but I was ready to start that journey.

As close as I was to my family, the move allowed me to figure out who I am without the pressures of second opinions. Being in a new environment gave me clarity on my beliefs, and while my views may have altered, I figured it out on my own. It was little moments like these that made me realize I was propelling myself out of the spoiled teenager life and into an independent young adult—and I was here for the ride.

I take pride in my purpose, being individualistic and independent, but there's still the cautious ride to avoid the bridge of self-destruction, intersecting the corner of Confidence Road and Cocky Avenue. Mapping out directions to stay humble but confident embodies inner strength, not just a protective exterior. Explaining your needs rather than demanding them steers you in the right direction. Family and friends may come along for joy rides from time to time but finding that inner GPS strength will positively impact not only you, but them as well.

It is important to remember not everyone takes the same road trip, so despite the positivity that identifying your inner self can bring, some negativity is likely to follow.

One day I was having a conversation with a woman I'd met a few times from work. She knew I was married and close to my family. I knew she was family-oriented and vocal with her opinions. On paper we seemed similar, but honestly those were the only similarities.

Finding ourselves standing next to each another in a parking lot during a fire alarm, we awkwardly started making obligatory small talk.

I turned to her and said, "How are your children?"

Her face lit up, and she started to speak in detail regarding their milestones.

In a lengthy, one-sided discussion, she updated me about her young children and their independent self-awareness. One had courageously defended herself against a bully, while the other had accomplished learning the alphabet with flying colors. When she proudly finished telling these stories, her beaming smile turned into a tight, crooked lip.

Staring at me with a look of frustration, her mood changed. She didn't say another word. Instead, she looked at me with a tilted head, squinted eyes, and a frown until we walked back inside a few minutes later. I stood there and immediately felt judged and perplexed at the sudden shift of her emotions. I had the impression she felt I couldn't relate to her excitement since I had chosen to not have children. Though engaged, maybe I wasn't fully swept up in the amazement or didn't appear as excited as her expectations defined. Her fixation on my child-free situation prevented her from understanding that my choice was not only courageous but independent—the same attributes she had praised her daughter for when she stood up to that bully.

Many people wonder how my life can feel fulfilled without a child. Perhaps people are confused by misunderstanding the difference between feeling fulfilled and being fulfilled. To me, those are two different scenarios. Feeling fulfilled is the perception, while being ful-filled is the reality. Though the differences between the two are subtle, they can provide monumental impacts. For example, take these two statements: "I feel excited" versus "I am excited." The first statement provides a feeling of emotion based on that moment, while the other statement describes the actual trait.

For me, the difference between feeling fulfilled and being fulfilled is easy: social media vs. reality. People talk about their one thousand friends on a social media platform and admire their photoshopped pictures, but these well-designed and staged posts are facades. They're putting on a show to convince others how wonderful their life is. That result is a feeling of fulfillment for them.

Don't get me wrong; not all social media posts are surface-level, and I cautiously remember that. There are shining examples of sincerity on these platforms that do define a fulfilled lifestyle and should not be undoubtedly characterized. The same way I feel someone should approach viewing my childless and fulfilled life.

For me, fulfillment involves focusing on my health, both physically and mentally. In times when I feel down, I make an effort to speak about it. I understand the importance of expression and muster up the courage to discuss. I can speak to my family, my husband, my friends, or even a professional. Maintaining a positive mental state is key. Sometimes I need to take personal time to get there, whether that means getting some alone time, going for a walk, or even enjoying a little retail therapy. It helps me understand that those moments are not only positive breaks but necessary.

Working can become strenuous and exhausting, but also rewarding and gratifying. By centralizing your life goals and working hard but smart, one can achieve internal fulfillment. Hard work and perseverance propelled my career and earned me each step up the success ladder. Failures, rejections, and skeptics inspired the strength to persevere and prove doubters, along with myself, wrong. Professionally, I experience growth with both industry knowledge and self-confidence. A lasting work ethic, humility, integrity, and respect are extremely fulfilling for me.

Fortunately, work is not the only thing that makes my life fulfilled. Confidence also plays a major role. Family, friends, coworkers, and acquaintances know I will speak my mind respectfully in conversations, debate a moment passionately when provoked, and advocate for right when the situation is wrong. They all know what they see is exactly what they'll get. But let's not confuse confidence with rudeness. It all stems back to that intersection of Confidence Road and Cocky Avenue. Being comfortable in my skin while cheerleading for my life should not constitute arrogance. Even when humility is practiced or idealism is explained, others may find it egotistical. Don't put your pom-poms away just yet. Instead, surround yourself with people who will be your champion and support you.

I am genuinely happy and satisfied with my decisions, my conquered fears, and the challenges I've accepted in life. If I were to die tomorrow, my life, though short, would have been great. Happiness, love, cultural exposure, stability, confidence, accomplishments, and empowerment are just a few descriptions of my fulfilled life. No regrets and no what ifs.

However, some women believe my life is not fulfilled because I don't have a child. That is the only experience they know and can relate to. At other times, people focus on my love for reality television and miss all the other attributes in my life, so it isn't a shock when people voice their concerns. They honestly believe I'm missing out because I don't have those valuable mother and child moments. I understand and appreciate their worry. Sure, I will miss the 3:00 a.m. feedings, changing poopy diapers, and schlepping a thousand luggage bags around for a weekend getaway.

All kidding aside, milestones such as feeling the baby kick, seeing the sonogram, or raising a child are considered life-defining moments. Though these experiences are indeed amazing, both Jim and I are at ease missing out on them. I do not yearn for motherhood. None of those moments send warm feelings to my heart or set off a radar in my mind. It all boils down to this: The moments parents deem important are simply not necessary in my life. Moments in life are what you make of them, and what is best for your situation is probably not ideal for mine.

My soul is content. I understand my circumstances. Despite concerns from others, I view this as a choice, not a sacrifice—a calculated decision based on my own personal milestones.

I have taken pregnancy tests, and each time I did, the negative result didn't bring sorrow, just pure relief. That emotion is acceptable and not just when you are considered too young or not ready to have a baby.

In my early thirties, happily married, established within my career, and financially stable, a moment of concern turned to pure relief for

Jim and me when the test indicator showed a negative symbol. We were able to continue living our lives as *we* intended—child free.

Whether vacationing in the Caribbean or living our best lives in Massachusetts, my husband and I have a tight relationship. Even though I feel it is apparent, many people wonder if it will be enough since I missed out on that special bond a child brings. The answer to that question is yes.

At a Fancy Food Show in Chicago, a vendor spoke to me about a new bonding agent for salad dressing. I was one of four women visiting the booth and the only person who didn't have a child.

Weird fact to encounter at a booth designed to discuss food ingredients, I know. So, how did I come across this information, you ask?

The vendor told us the bonding agent was organic, non-GMO, and healthy. Her pitch focused on the product's kid-healthy formula, and voilà, the conversation shifted from ingredients to the formulation for a happy life with children.

Now, I fully understand you sell to specific segments and attract an audience, but I was not prepared for the befriending to come. Each person identified themselves by their name, the company they worked for, and how many children they had.

The first woman in line introduced herself with a smile.

"Hi, my name is Shelly, and I work for Kellogg. My kids, ages six and ten, are not the biggest fans of healthy food, but I am trying to get them to explore new trends."

The next woman in line introduced herself.

"Hi, my name is Lisa, and I am a flavor technician for Del Monte. I work with vegetables, so my kids are learning the importance of vegetables and appreciate the taste."

Next mother to speak, come on down!

"Hi, my name is Barb, and I am a director of innovation. My children are older, but they need to eat more salad."

It was now my turn to introduce myself. Knowing full well I couldn't add a child analogy into my introduction, I was anxious to see how this would unfold.

"Hi, my name is Danielle. I am an associate scientist at Cadbury Adams. I'm interested in how this new bonding agent would work, particularly in gum or gelatinous-based confections," I nerdly stated.

Awkward pause from everyone.

I knew this would happen. All of them were waiting to see if my introduction was over. The wonderment of if I have children and then the weird silence when they realized I wasn't going to address the topic ruined the momentum because I only talked business.

Insert mock disappointment music—*whomp, whomp, whomp.*

After what seemed like an eternal pause, the vendor looked directly at me. She briefly mentioned that the ingredient was more focused on liquid-based formulations. She then turned to the other women to discuss more about their children. I stayed to listen because I was curious to learn about the ingredient, but I sensed the topic of children was not done.

And then it happened.

"Danielle, do you have any children?" the vendor asked, staring directly at me.

All eyes focused on me, waiting in anticipation.

"No," I quickly said, shaking my head with a slight grin and looking straight at the vendor.

"Oh, that's OK," the vendor said while looking down at her pamphlet. This was the first time she didn't look directly at me.

Talk about awkwardness!

How was I supposed to react to her "*OK*"? Thanks? Thank you for telling me it is OK I don't have children?

Instead, I stood with those women, embarrassed and simply wanting to understand how the agent bonds, but the awkwardness didn't end there. When I brought up the bonding agent again, all the women heard was the word "bond." Conversations started around their growing and changing bonds with their children.

Barb addressed me before speaking. "I do hope you are able to experience the amount of joy and bond in life like we have with our children."

"Thank you," I replied. I knew they were wishing me their interpretation of pure bliss, but a simple "thank you" was the most genuine response I could give.

And for those wondering, to this day I have no idea what the heck that bonding agent was.

Some people worry that the life I chose will not be enough in the future. Sure, I might need some other type of bond, but there is no guarantee a child would provide it. Is it so terrible for me to say the bond I have with myself is enough? Because it is. I know exactly who I am and what I want, and I don't feel the need to apologize for my special bond with myself. Most importantly, I know that when I get hangry a simple Snickers bar isn't going to cut it.

As author Margaret Young wrote, "You must first be who you really are, then do what you need to do, in order to have what you want."[7] Even if I didn't have my husband or my great family, I know that the bond I have with myself is strong enough to take on life independently. Yes, taking on life with a partner or family adds a rich layer, but I am not debating that. Instead, I am making sure that those who question my decisions understand that the bond I have with myself is central to who I am, and it's unbreakable.

You don't need to fit in; you just need to find out who you are. Aristotle states, "Knowing yourself is the beginning of all wisdom when the actuality of thought is life." I don't need to be like you, and you definitely can't be like me. If having a child defines and completes your purpose, that's amazing. On the flip side, if not having a child is your life plan, that's amazing as well. There isn't just one correct answer to purpose.

When I look in the mirror, the person looking back at me has no doubt who she is, and that to me is the main way I define *my* awesome purpose in life.

---

7   Brene Brown, *The Gifts Of Imperfection* (Hazelden Publishing, 2010),

Chapter 2
DISAPPOINTMENT

"Are you afraid of disappointing your family, society, or even God?"

Has anyone ever told you, "I'm not mad; I'm just really disappointed"?

Those words hollow out my stomach with uncomfortable scenarios to face.

If you happen to be dealing with someone who is seasoned with laying on the guilt— like my Italian mother, passive-aggressive bosses, or adorable-eyed nephews—words aren't even needed. A stare will do. Honestly, just thinking about that stare defeats me.

I wish they would just yell instead.

We've all experienced negative emotions that swell up when we're disappointed, sometimes leading to depression, sadness, or isolation. Rather than face that kind of negativity, we avoid situations that risk disappointment. Doing this causes us to adjust our expectations, compromise goals, and risk losing self-awareness. This emotional baggage comes with a carry-on bag of regret, and not the kind that contains travel-sized toiletries, magazines, or snacks, just physical ailments.

When chronically experienced, disappointment can result in digestive disorders, depressed immune systems, and a strain on the heart.[1]

All things considered, I would be OK if the airline lost this piece of luggage.

It is common for people to question my family's reaction when I told them I didn't want children. Did I let them down? Were they angry, sad, or disappointed? Were they expecting a different decision? If my family settled for my choice, were friends discouraged or disheartened by the news? What about the fear of disappointing God?

With such a personal discussion, a light tone is often easier than a complicated biography. A punchy go-to response such as, "Disappoint my family yet again? Nope!" is how I respond.

If they offer a smile or a laugh in return, I am more willing to detail my life choices; however, a disgusted reaction suggests this person has already judged me. Nothing I say will matter. During these moments, I try to confidently walk away while reminding myself that their negativity will not influence my behavior.

While waiting in an airport on my first business trip with a new company, I was sitting with a coworker, Sara. She didn't have children yet instantly started a conversation around kids.

"Do you have kids?" she asked.

"No," I replied.

Staring directly at me with a look of despair, she quickly asked, "Is your family disappointed about that?"

Her tone and abruptness concerned me. I stared at her for a moment while gathering my thoughts.

"Disappointed?" I asked, tilting my head. "Because I don't have children? No."

Contemplating her immediate response, I assumed Sara was feeling the pressure to have children and needed advice. I found myself in

---

1   Jayden Mathews, "Effects of Disappointment," *Classroom*, https://classroom. synonym.com/effects-disappointment-8285964.html.

unfamiliar territory—finally not being judged but doing the judging. It was possible I was incorrectly reading the room, but with her eyes locked in my direction, I sensed she felt some sort of pressure.

To ease the tension, I answered with a dollop of humor. "If my parents or family are disappointed with my decision to not have children, they do a great job hiding it."

Sara did not bat an eyelash. Her serious look of concern dominated the mood. I quickly pivoted from the humorous approach to offer a sincere answer.

I began explaining my relationship with my family. "My family and I are very close and vocal. They were aware of my decision to not have children because I had upfront conversations with them."

Sara simply replied, "Oh." She looked defeated and sad.

I continued to explain the importance of communication and acknowledged how difficult it can be when forced, especially with family. It was necessary to remind Sara that without discussion, unique and individual beliefs are not expressed, which allows others to assume their thoughts are universal. After we spoke, another colleague arrived at the gate. Sara politely said hello but was quiet for the remainder of the trip, which gave me the impression she was deeply in thought about our conversation and remained conflicted.

Was it wrong of me to feel helpless for Sara but grateful for my situation? I couldn't relate to her in the way she wanted, but I couldn't stop thinking about it. Clearly my family's acceptance was fortunate. Besides providing Sara guidance to openly communicate, I was not sure what else I could do to advise her. I wanted to hug her and whisper that everything was going to be OK.

Maybe I should have?

Maybe that was exactly what she needed.

Instead, I worried that action would focus attention on Sara from the other coworkers. But honestly, the biggest prevention of the hug was because I didn't believe everything would be OK. How could I? I barely knew Sara, let alone her family.

Shortly after this trip, she left the company and we lost contact. Based on my impression, I'll bet Sara succumbed to family pressure and has children now. Hopefully, she's living a happy life.

As the youngest of three daughters, my personality reflects both my mom, Catherine, and my dad, Donald. I have the patience of my dad (none), the mental strength of my mom, and a nice balance of German and Italian characteristics. Basically, I talk with my hands, I love with my soul, and I will fight you if you hurt anyone I love.

Mom and Dad raised my sisters and me to live a life based on our vision. To be honest, if I had a child out of fear of letting Donald and Catherine down, they would be disappointed with themselves. My parents made it very clear that I am not in this world to live up to their expectations, and they are not in this world to live up to mine.

It is important to make your expectations known to the people impacted by them and to thoroughly consider what is best for yourself. Communicate openly. Deciding not to have children was not a rash or spur-of-the-moment decision; it was a calculated and difficult one that I discussed multiple times around my family. With such a personal topic, a typical "one and done" conversation wasn't enough—not even in my household where I was lucky enough to avoid the added stress of disappointment. Instead, discussions of independence, overall concerns, motherhood stories, and affirmation occurred.

Dad encouraged me to make the most of my life. Initially, my mom doubted my decision would last, based on her own experience. Mama Schwartz was a person destined to have children, yet she understood it was my decision. Thankfully, she oozes acceptance, understanding, and support. She never insinuated my decision was wrong or forced her ideals onto me. Instead, she listened and appreciated my belief by openly talking to her friends about my decision and advocated for authenticity. If I encountered a particularly unnerving moment discussing my childless decision, venting to my mom was an outlet. She heeded the conversation and always reminded me that *my* decision does not owe society an explanation. That type of reassurance detailed her acceptance, but more importantly, her willingness to support my choice directly in society's face.

My sisters knew I marched to the beat of my own drum, and my thought process was no surprise. Actually, my sister Dorene thought I was going to become a nun since I never missed Sunday school, church, or a confessional. She believed that was my destined path. Truth is, my mom made the rules. She never missed church, so her youngest child did not either.

I guess Dorene's beat was off tempo!

The most synchronized march and rhythm came with my in-laws' blunt reaction. Jim and I decided to tell his parents we didn't want children. So one night at dinner, Jim casually mentioned it. I sat there awkwardly waiting for a response. The anticipation was killing me.

After a few seconds, which felt like an eternity to me, Jim's father stopped eating, looked up with a straight face and said, "Smart."

Without breaking stride while eating her noodles, Jim's mother nodded in agreement.

Jim is an only child, and based on their one-sided response, I jokingly assumed my husband drove them to that conclusion—even though I know he didn't.

Jim's parents are first-generation, hard-working, middle-class people. They enjoy the very simple things in life, are not afraid of challenges, are always emotionally grounded, and are selective with people and conversations. Purposefully quiet and quintessentially stoic, their quick response to our baby-free conversation accurately represented James' and Susan's personalities.

The conversation around kids ended right there. At no time did they pressure us, ask additional questions, or provide more opinions. Instead, they never said a word, knowing that keeping up with Jim was now my problem, not theirs.

I'm kidding. Jim is not a problem. I have known Jim for over half my life, and he is my best friend. I wouldn't have it any other way.

I met Jim in my sophomore year of college. He traveled down

to West Virginia University with his best friend, who was dating my roommate Jennifer—who, by the way, is still my bestie!

It wasn't love at first sight, more like annoyance at first encounter. I lived in a dorm where you needed a key to get into the front entrance. Jim didn't have a key, but he did have the ability to bang on the door at seven thirty in the morning. I remember waking up furious and thinking this chaos had better be because the building was on fire. Nope. It was just Jim stopping by to see his best friend, Hector. Not being a morning person, I greeted him with a "what the hell do you want stare" instead of a friendly smile. He introduced himself and quickly realized his intro meant nothing at 7:30 a.m. After I had time to wake up and my coffee had settled in, we all hung out and got to know one another. Jim and I realized that we are both from New Jersey and lived twenty-five miles from each other. He made me laugh; the conversations were effortless, and no matter where we were or what we were doing, we always had a great time. However, I saw us just as friends. I was dating someone at the time, and Jim was too.

We kept in touch after he traveled back to New Jersey, and when I came home for the Christmas holiday, we made it a point to meet up. Returning back for my second semester, I started to see Jim as more than a friend. I missed him and wanted to explore something more than friendship.

When spring break came around, I didn't go to Florida or party it up in Vegas. Instead, I went back to New Jersey to see my family and ask Jim out. Luckily for me, he wanted a relationship too, and the rest is history.

It's funny how life works.

I moved six and a half hours away from New Jersey to West Virginia in order to meet my future husband, who ironically lived only twenty minutes away from my childhood home. Sometimes basic coincidences turn into life-altering decisions.

That decision to start dating completely shifted my life. I found someone who listened to my voice, enjoyed my company, accepted my authentic self, and kept me balanced. We complement each other very well; he is passive, and I am aggressive. If we are in a crowd, all moving toward one destination, I am the one in front with elbows paving the way, usually missing everything around me. Jim, on the other hand, stays behind, cautiously surveying the area at a slower pace. Throughout our time together, though, our personalities have rubbed off on one another. He still needs to remind me that not everyone wants a fight, just like I need to remind him you sometimes need to put up a fight. Like people in every relationship, we argue, but usually about money or—according to him—how to correctly load a dishwasher.

One thing we do agree on is how great we are at communicating. Communication is key, and with consistent communication there is no room for disappointment. We began communicating early. When Jim and I were starting to become serious, we had talks about the future. Even though I could see myself married to Jim, children were not part of the equation for me. He had a right to know how I felt. At the time I wasn't sure what his stance was on kids, so the buildup to this conversation was intense. I knew that if we were on different paths, I could lose the guy I love.

The first conversation I had with Jim was over the phone five months into our relationship. I was a sophomore in college so the beginning of our relationship was long distance. Back then we didn't have the technological features like Zoom or Facetime to intimately connect. Instead, the world was being introduced to dial-up internet, AOL chat, and cell phones small enough to fit in a large purse.

Being timid and scared, I did not approach the conversation with finesse. In a moment of silence, not knowing how to approach the situation, I simply blurted out, "Jim, I don't think I want to have children in the future."

There was a moment of silence, and again I filled it by correcting my statement.

"Actually, I don't think . . . I *know* I don't want to have children in the future."

"OK," Jim said right away.

I didn't hear a hesitation, a cracked voice, or an undertone to his response, which I took as him being sincere.

"I'm young, so my feelings might change, but I don't see that happening," I said firmly.

That truthful caveat was added for me, not him. Since I was young, it ensured opportunities for the future. It was not intended to ease Jim's mind or decision.

"I don't want kids. It is not a priority for me," he said matter-of-factly.

"Are you sure?" I asked.

"Yes. It wasn't something I thought about."

"Maybe you should. I don't want you to realize later on you wanted kids. I think you should take some time to really think about what I am stating. I am telling you I don't want a family that would be considered *ours*," I emphasized.

With discussions like this, time is an important factor. I'd had my whole life to consider, understand, and determine this decision, whereas Jim had five minutes. Though he seemed content and accepting, it was necessary to allow him to process this reality. Jim was calm, rational, and definitive. He sounded sincere, but how could I know for sure over the phone after one conversation? All I knew was relief that we'd had the discussion, and a small sense of reassurance he felt the same way.

Shortly after this truth-bomb I had to get off the phone. The mood was upbeat and loving, not solemn or awkward. We briefly changed the subject to my dreaded midterm and ended with our typical, "Love you!"

Maybe he was being truthful, I thought, and children weren't a priority?

The next day we had our second phone conversation on this topic. Oddly enough, the discussion started off the same as always: two best friends happy to hear from one another. I was expecting a different tone based on the bomb I had dropped; however, Jim was the one who brought up the topic this time.

"I am fine with no children," he calmly said.

"Are you sure?" I said again, questioning his response.

"Yes. I don't have that urge or feeling to want or need kids," he affirmed.

"Are you saying this because you think it is what I want to hear?" I asked.

"I know you, Danielle. If someone were saying something because they thought that was what you wanted to hear, you would sense that bullshit right out the gate," he stated.

He's right. I can sense BS from a mile away. Especially when it's directed toward me.

"It will only be us. There will be no legacy or traditions to pass on," I said.

"Why, are we not enough?" he asked.

That comment provided me with the first substantial feeling that Jim was processing reality and was OK with it.

"We are," I responded.

"I know we are," he confidently answered.

Jim then changed topics.

Trusting he would be honest and talk to me if needed, I believed his decision; though in my mind, something of this magnitude should be discussed in person.

Three months after our initial conversation he planned a visit. During this time, I took the opportunity to discuss the baby topic. Over dinner, sitting in my dorm room, I casually asked his certainty about not having children. He stopped eating, looked straight into my eyes and said, "Yes. I don't care about having children. It is honestly not important to me."

That was it. That look was the final confirmation I needed to believe children were not a factor in *his* journey either.

Those multiple discussions raised key questions and concerns that needed to be addressed. Was he saying this to make me happy? Was he afraid he'd lose me if he didn't feel the same as me? Did he fully understand what he was giving up? Had he realized it would only be me and him in the future? Something as important as this deserves attention, intention, and understanding from both sides.

Tough dialogues like this illustrate living a life of your own design while inviting others into it. It is one thing to have the confidence to approach a given subject, quite another to actively engage in discussions to determine clear direction. Luckily for me, Jim was on the No Kids Express as well.

I am blessed to be in a situation where I can have open conversations with the most important people in my life. Having this good fortune does make my child-free journey less complicated. With their genuine concern and encouragement, it's easy to include my family for important discussions. I would be foolish not to. My mom supports her children and beams with pride when highlighting her daughters' strengths. Both Dawn and Dorene show determination and resilience in raising their autistic children. Facing each day with adversity and sacrifice, they provide a balance of flexibility and mental toughness. Admittedly, it is something my mom would have struggled with. But though she has never experienced having a child with a disability, my mom always listens and provides guidance during difficult moments.

Even in those moments when my mom does not agree with the parenting approach, my sisters know she is a concrete source of comfort. For me, she is proud of my tenacity to be true to myself. She admires my drive to try new opportunities while encouraging me to never lose that ambition. Mom and Dad instilled outstanding integrity and strength, and I keep their motivation close to my heart.

Another laudable example of support from my family occurred shortly after my father's death. Jim and I started a different chapter in life and moved from the fast-paced, aggressive East Coast to the calm, friendly Midwest. We left our family, the friends we have known for years, familiarity, and home so I could pursue a new career opportunity and challenge my professional scientific growth at Georgia Pacific in Appleton, Wisconsin. Jim had confidence in my success, even though we had no guarantees. Since we knew nothing about Wisconsin or anyone there, the adjustment raised concerns. Would we be able to establish friendships? Would the environment feel comfortable enough for both of us to call it a second home? Would I be a success? What would happen if moving a thousand miles from family and friends was a mistake? Not only would I disappoint Jim but also myself.

If I'd had a child adding to those complex worries, my decision would have been much harder with the possibility of a different outcome.

The only reassuring encouragement I received on moving to Wisconsin was through the constant in-person discussions I had with my mom, sisters, and brothers-in-law. I honestly didn't say much during those moments; I simply listened and soaked in their words of affirmation.

My mother consistently mentioned how proud my dad was of me while he looked down from heaven, ensuring his presence was still a significant part of the family. The same would hold true for me, a thousand miles away. I wasn't abandoning the family; instead I was acquiring more culture, life, and experiences through an opportunity that I had earned. Their proud messages highlighting my driving force and courage gave me confidence. I am also grateful they acknowledged how the move would be difficult and sad for everyone. This forced inevitable emotions to the surface that had to be confronted head-on before allowing them to become excuses.

Despite all the encouragement, my father's death still presented a mental dilemma. It seemed too soon to leave, as though I was running away from my grief or abandoning my family. I felt lost and disappointed in myself for even thinking about leaving. Desperate, I asked my dad to provide a sign.

I got two.

The first sign happened a few hours later when I was driving the usual route home from work. I stopped at the intersection and looked to the left for oncoming traffic. I then looked to the right, and my eyes grew wide with amazement. I gasped. Next to the stop sign stood a tall bright blue sign that said GEORGIA PACIFIC with an arrow pointing to the right. Never before had I seen that sign. It seemed as though it were a literal and metaphorical notice from Dad that I was meant to work at Georgia Pacific. I was a little spooked but reassured.

I also felt an impatient blast from the car horn behind me.

A few days later, the second sign was even more unbelievable. It happened after a lunch discussion with Jim and my close friend, Arnel, about our potential move to Wisconsin. I had told Arnel about the sudden appearance of the Georgia Pacific sign. When we left the restaurant, I sat in the back seat of my jeep, Jim rode shotgun, and Arnel drove down Cedar Lane in Teaneck, New Jersey. We pulled up to a traffic light, still chatting.

Jim and Arnel abruptly stopped.

"Guys, do you see that?" Arnel asked.

"Holy shit, YES!" Jim stated in astonishment.

"WHAT?" I leaned forward, and Arnel pointed to the radio dashboard in my jeep.

In a big, bold font, it stated: "**APPLETON**." The city of our potential move. A city I had never heard of until this job opportunity with Georgia Pacific presented itself.

What was even more bizarre was when a song began playing on the radio: T. J. Miller's "Appleton."

A song about Appleton, Wisconsin.

Phenomenal and uncanny.

After the shock wore off, Jim and I decided to make the move.

Living in the Midwest sparked new in-depth conversations around my choice to not have children. The Midwest provided a culture shock to this East Coast tornado. Typically, my home area is fast-paced, unfriendly, blunt, and selective. We are outspoken, diverse, and gritty. Upon moving to Wisconsin, I quickly realized my unfriendly, guarded demeanor was extremely intimidating to all the friendly Midwesterners.

The first week we moved into our house, our neighbor introduced himself.

With a smile and a very inviting handshake, he greeted us. "Hi, welcome to the neighborhood. If you need anything, my garage door is always open."

Confused already by his way of introducing himself, I cautiously shook his hand and said, "Hello. You really leave the garage door open for anyone?"

Still smiling and shaking my hand, he enthusiastically said, "YES! We all do."

Living on the East Coast, you don't even leave your door open for your family members.

Perplexed and weary of trusting him, I simply said, "OK. I won't do that, but thanks for letting me know."

He was a little thrown off by my blunt tone but was nonetheless always pleasant throughout the six years I lived next door.

And that is the Midwest I experienced: pleasant, friendly, and trusting, with a passion to enjoy life and the Green Bay Packers.

I did find the area I lived in to be less diverse, having an infinity for passive-aggressive behavior and communication, with a much slower-paced environment and outspoken views around religion.

I generally found myself discussing the correlation between disappointment and religion more frequently there. A handful of people expressed concern that my decision to not have children would dissatisfy God. For them, God provided us life to live and procreate. If they were to engage in a child-free life, they would draw constant scrutiny upon themselves, believing God was disappointed with their decision. The majority of these conversations were pleasant, with the participants acknowledging a child as a unique gift from God. They respected my opinions. Common curiosities and questions provoked discussions ranging from a fear of distress to a sense of intrigue and respect. What typically started out as discussions about children usually pivoted to explanations of religious symbolism. Listening to some practicing

Jewish colleagues detail Hanukkah in regard to the Maccabean Revolt, or learning about the denominations within the Mormon religion, provided a necessary view versus glorified sensationalism. There's more to those religions than eight small gifts, lighted candles, and living within a community in Utah. When others assume they understand my life without a child, it provides another great example of where generalizations do not provide clear pictures. Instead, it emphasizes the need to not judge a book by its cover—even if that book is the *Bible*, *The Book of Mormon*, or the *Tanakh*.

Though most religious conversations were enlightening, some were disturbing.

At a company picnic, I was introduced to a coworker's family, including her sister and nine nieces and nephews. The children were full of energy and bonded with other kids at the picnic while the sister quietly focused on her children.

My coworker Vanessa, an extrovert who is the life of the party, stood next to her introverted sister Amanda during the picnic. Though Amanda was timid and soft spoken, we had small, friendly conversations throughout the day. As the day went on, one particular incident changed the tone of our interaction.

"Do you have any children?" Amanda sweetly asked me.

"No," I replied.

"Are you Catholic?" she asked.

Surprised, I hesitated. "I am but not practicing."

"So, you are Catholic, don't practice the religion, are married, and do not have children, correct?" she exclaimed in an aggressive tone.

Thoroughly confused at the direction this conversation was taking, I simply raised my eyebrow and said, "Yes."

"You know you are disappointing God. How do you feel about disappointing God?" she angrily asked.

My face froze.

Numb and not knowing how to answer, I turned to what I always feel comfortable with: humor.

"I'm bummed out!" I shrugged my shoulders and smiled.

She didn't even smirk. We stood there in silence. I was awkwardly uncomfortable while she was angrily waiting for a response or an apology. Honestly, I didn't know what she wanted. After a minute of loud silence, I was tired from being on trial.

"Nice to meet you," I said while walking away.

During the rest of the picnic, I kept a fair distance away from her. Unfortunately, that meant distancing myself from Vanessa as well. This was a shame since Vanessa's character always brought enjoyable entertainment. Luckily, my encounter with Amanda did not change Vanessa's opinion toward me. We continued to have the same work relationship afterward.

Religion is an extremely delicate discussion point. Though I understand my ignorance, I also acknowledge my own beliefs. Since I am aware this topic is sensitive, aggressive conversations cause me to stumble with my thoughts and become closed off.

When confronted by people who feel God is angered by my choice, I usually say nothing. On rare occasions when I do respond, it is a simple statement explaining how God forgives. I say that not because I am looking for God's forgiveness, but because I know it is a universally accepted notion across all religions. Taking the opportunity to remind people of God's most admirable quality is my last attempt to remind others of sacred humanity.

Unfortunately, based on past experiences with these belligerent situations, my feelings are never taken into consideration. Knowing how exhausted I am from debating *my* choices, I have no desire to engage in a religious one. The best option seems to be morally walking away.

Disappointment is a loaded emotion. It can prevent you from becoming the best version of yourself while potentially causing you to miss opportunities. "To be able to navigate life successfully, so that you make the best decision for yourself at any given moment, you need to be authentic—you need to be able to counter external influences pulling you to go against the grain of your own gut feelings."[2]

Though sometimes letting others down is inevitable, one should remember that whether it be God or anyone else, there are two possibilities why someone would be disappointed in you: They either don't share your view, or they have the wrong expectations.

---

2   Stephen Joseph, *Authentic: How To Be Yourself and Why It Matters* (London: Piatkus, 2016).

Chapter 3
MATERIALISTIC & SUPERFICIAL

"Are you afraid of getting fat?"

Do you find yourself staring at the phone checking your latest social media post for new likes or comments? Maybe you are too attached to your new designer splurge? Perhaps you feel inferior when someone close owns something nicer than you? All these questions sound common and innocent, but what if I told you they are associated with attributes identifying materialistic people?[1]

Would you automatically accept that definition, or defend your behavior?

People assume my life starts off with hard work and ends with champagne. Although that sounds amazing, it isn't necessarily true. Yes, I work hard, and sometimes I celebrate life in the manner of a cocktail or three at the end of the day, but my life is not a bubbly celebration of stress-free adventures simply because I don't have a child. I am fully aware my life may look easier in some respects, but that doesn't mean I'm not emotionally or physically struggling in life. Last time I checked, many of my friends who have children also own stock

---

1   Rebecca Crespo, "17 Signs of a Materialistic Person," *Minimalism Made Simple*, July 2021, https://www.minimalismmadesimple.com/home/materialistic-person/.

in Bottle King or Wine Emporium—which is phenomenal.

With the perception of an easier life, being defined as materialistic or superficial follow. Between being asked if I have no desire to give up drinking to whether I have a possible fear of becoming fat during pregnancy, these examples illustrate predetermined judgments of my life. Sometimes those exterior claims made me wonder what type of vibes I was sending out. That contemplation proved vibes were not the issue, just the common battle of assumptions versus *my* reality.

Once, on a work trip, I was patiently waiting at a rental car counter and saw a woman who was agitated because her reservation was incorrect on the app. You could hear the desperation in her voice while on the phone with her husband, frantically searching for a car large enough for her family. She paused for a moment, and for some odd reason I felt compelled to talk to her.

"Are you on vacation?" I politely asked.

She sighed with exhaustion and stress. "Yes. Are you?"

Quickly matching her sigh, I said, "No, work travel."

"Do you have children?" she pleasantly inquired.

From her previous phone conversation, I knew she had children, but I wanted to seem oblivious, so I simply replied, "No, do you?"

From that question, she was very forthcoming about her life. "I have four children, and I am a yoga instructor. I own a yoga studio in Arizona."

This woman was physically fit and extremely personable. She also understood the need for relaxation and business separation, given our destination was Memphis. Feeling her empowerment and the success of owning a business, I was impressed.

"That is amazing! Congratulations on owning your own business."

Not knowing a lot about yoga, I wanted to learn more about the field and her entrepreneurship. This was also the perfect opportunity to discuss if goat yoga simply involves goats roaming around your personal space while mastering the downward dog position. Unfortunately for me, her practice did not involve goats, so instead, she detailed the importance of the mind and body.

Starting yoga as an escape from reality, she had quickly realized the skill was an essential tool to conquer life. It was fascinating listening to her describe the different techniques to ease emotional and physical pains, along with some of her clients' backstories. According to her, simple poses, such as the child's pose with manageable breathing, are an easy way to support relaxation, conquer depression, and promote inner peace. She also suggested the importance of movement-intensive practices to propel flow. Again, not knowing anything about yoga, I allowed her to dominate the conversation with her knowledge and passion.

The early yoga classes she attended were made up of new moms with the common desire to escape and shift their mental body image. The group of women felt the pressure to bounce back to pre-baby weight.

Why wouldn't they?

From societal influences, social media platforms, celebrity postpartum progress, to your basic mommy and me class, there are standard pressures staring from all directions. Not to mention the worst pressure of all—yourself.

Pregnancy and childbirth are associated with dramatic changes in a woman's body, which some mothers perceive negatively. Research shows body dissatisfaction nine months postpartum is greater than all pregnancy trimesters for some, resulting in depression, eating/appetite abnormalities, greater weight gain, and other psychological health issues.[2]

Most of my new acquaintance's clients were frightened or disappointed with their mirror image, so she wanted to help advocate for the importance of body satisfaction through the physical and mental state of yoga. She went on to explain how some journeys are more difficult due to the clients' "unrecognizable, defeated, or disgusted" reflections of themselves. With all that pressure, superficial labels and

2   Dwenda Gjerdingen et al., "Predictors of Mothers' Postpartum Body Dissatisfaction," *Women's Health* 49, no. 6 (Sept. 2009): 491–504.

lack of leniency dangled over their conscience, preventing many of them from having a second child.

I never considered that a person might not have a child based on a concern about body image, let alone someone who's already had a child. I've heard stories of women contemplating pregnancy based on the pain and complications labor delivers; however, listening to my new friend's mission, it is easy to understand how one develops an image from a critical self-lens. There are various forms and levels of body dysmorphic disorder triggered by numerous reasons, including postpartum baby weight.

When you have body dysmorphic disorder, you intensely focus on your appearance and body image to the point where it impacts your daily functions. Preoccupied beliefs of a flaw or defect in your appearance create actions designed to fix or hide that perceived issue. From excessive weight loss tactics to invasive cosmetic surgery, males and females of all ages attempt to solve their body image only to temporarily reduce the distress. By trying to alleviate a preconceived body image, one might experience anxiety, severe depression, or even suicidal thoughts and behaviors.[3]

The instructor witnessed all situations through her clients' experiences and partnered with a professional psychiatrist for those who needed additional support.

Typing this out with my glass of diet soda and cookie next to me, I am lucky enough to say my body image and self-consciousness were never reasons to not have children. Am I that self-assured with my physical appearance that I have no insecurities? Heck no! I honestly dread the summer now that I'm in my forties. It's too hot to wear long sleeves, and for some reason I'm gaining all my weight in my arms. Besides the bottom skin flapping back and forth and having its own conversation, I now have large fat deposits on my biceps. Sometimes I don't feel as confident when these fat deposits are dominant, forcing

---

3   Mayo Clinic. "Body Dysmorphic Disorder," http://www.mayoclinic.org/diseases-conditions/body-dysmorphic-disorder/symptoms-causes/syc-20353938#.

me to spend more time contemplating what to wear out in public.

Although it might seem this body image ruins my summers, it doesn't. What it boils down to is having consistent love and acceptance of my five-foot-two self—including the enhanced love handles that somehow show up even when I just smell a potato chip. To be clear, when I look at those love handles, do they bother me? Occasionally. Just not enough to prevent me from eating those delicious Ruffles potato chips again! Considering I'm willing to amplify those love handles in exchange for tastiness, the same embrace would occur if I were pregnant. Nevertheless, my desire for snack food runs much deeper than my desire for having a child.

Oh, and before I forget, goat yoga is legitimately real live goats hanging out while you contort your mind and body. If I were to do goat yoga, I am positive those goats would be preoccupied eating the snacks out of my yoga bag!

Since we're talking about the tasty nourishment of Ruffles potato chips, let it be known those ridges of perfection are washed down with a cold Sam Adams from time to time. I don't drink every day, so I am taken back when people ask or even assume alcohol was a reason for my child-free decision. I'm guessing there are people who consider liquor a reason to avoid parenthood, but why am I lumped into that group? Just because I responsibly enjoy an adult beverage from time to time does not mean it consumes my life—nor am I ashamed of that enjoyment. This mindset poses a larger question—would anyone be excited to give up something they enjoy? Probably not, but you sacrifice if necessary. Especially if that necessity will bring you more joy in life.

Ironically, I was having a discussion about children with an older gentleman who was sitting by himself at a crowded bar. There was a small area with an open seat next to him.

"Is this seat taken?" I asked.

He looked up at me, moved his seat over a few inches to the left and said, "No" in a monotone voice.

Even though his disposition wasn't the most inviting, I felt it was necessary to initiate small talk in a fairly crowded bar.

"Thank you for making room at the bar for me. I appreciate it," I said.

"Why are you by yourself?" he bluntly asked.

"I am waiting for my coworkers. We had an exceedingly long day at work and needed to unwind," I answered.

The bar was small and dimly lit, and it smelled like stale beer and bad decisions. I don't quite remember how the topic of children came up, but in line with his blunt personality, he made an interesting statement.

Staring at the bowl of pretzels, he grumpily asked, "You enjoy happy hours?"

Uncomfortable because of his tone, I avoided eye contact and hoped he would get the hint. "Yes, sometimes they are needed after hard days."

He didn't get the hint.

Moving his focus from the pretzels to my face, he declared, "Happy hours seem more important to you than being a good mom!"

Here we go again. The societal assumption that a female is, or wants, to be a mother was in full effect. Mentally screaming profanities, all I could do was answer truthfully. "No. I am not a mom."

Not to outdo himself, he quickly provided more interesting wisdom. "Just for your information, you can do both when that time comes. Enjoy your hard work with a beer during happy hour while being a mom."

His comments were genuine, but yet again rashly irrelevant.

Completely done with this conversation, I sarcastically rolled my eyes. "Cool, thanks."

Not appreciating that response, he repositioned himself in the chair, placed his glass firmly down and detailed his explanation. "I'm serious. I raised my children in bars. My wife and I would bring our children into bars that had video games and televisions, so we didn't have to purchase those luxuries for them. My wife and I would enjoy our beverages and entertainment as well."

Listening to what he was saying, something switched inside me. Maybe he wasn't being stubborn and just . . . genuine? Although his communication style didn't support his messaging, I still realized in a roundabout way that he wasn't wrong.

My generation is referred to as latchkey kids—parents needed to both hold jobs, so the children latched house keys to their book bags, allowing them to enter an empty house. Television was the babysitter, and meals prepped the night before were in the refrigerator with heating instructions.

During the early and mid-nineties, there were no after school programs, which forced children to independently care for themselves while the adults worked. This practice created a generation who experienced different effects than previous generations did when they were young. From loneliness, fear, and peer pressure susceptibility to successful independent sustainability, latchkey experiences influenced adolescent growth. Research also indicates that women of latchkey children suffer from guilt and negative psychological reactions, impacting their daily lives.[4]

Circling back to the man at the bar, his point had validity. Replace your childhood home that babysat you with cartoons and video games with a bar offering the same thing—essentially you have a similar scenario. Except with his circumstance, both parents were present, and he seemingly did not have negative effects from their tactics.

A few years later I was visiting a manufacturing plant where a coworker was speaking to line operators. She was discussing the family wedding she had recently attended, from the beautiful church ceremony to the "distasteful" reception celebration with alcohol. As

---

4   J. Rajalakshmi and P. Thanasekaren, "The Effects and Behaviors of Home Alone Situation by Latchkey Children," *American Journal of Nursing Science* 4, no. 4 (August 2015).

I walked in halfway through the conversation, she was emphatically describing how disgraceful alcohol is. Normally I respect and listen to people's beliefs, but when preaching is involved, it becomes harder to show attentiveness (and she was a "preacher").

"You understand alcohol clouds your judgment of life? The miracle of life is impacted by the Devil Juice!" she protested.

Finding her lecture not only entertaining but one-sided, I just stared at her with a smirk on my face.

Continuing to push her ideologies on me, she focused her attention more on my connection to alcohol. "If you can't separate the need for alcohol, you are weak. It is probably a good thing you didn't bring a child into the world!"

Everyone stood there, frozen and in shock, including me. I'm assuming their quiet expressions were directly related to her abusive comments toward me.

I just walked away. Not because her comment struck a chord—quite the opposite. It was insignificant.

As crazy as this sounds, there are people with these beliefs who have no issue lecturing, sometimes unprovoked. From my encounters, I've learned that these mindsets are guarded, one-sided, fully judgmental, and unapologetic. Engaging a discussion on your individualistic point of view would be useless, because these people are not listening to you. They have no desire to know you yet have no issue claiming unrealistic points. Successfully ignoring their perspective and walking away has been shown to be the best debate.

Walking away from ignorant instances can be difficult. The same can be said about sacrifices. I see my pregnant friends genuinely look envious when I have a drink in my hand. Sometimes they have even asked me to order and consume their favorite cocktail. Of course, I need to know which drink I am agreeing to before I say yes. I might love my friends, but I draw that love at Jägermeister.

Keep in mind that it's much easier telling someone to walk away from a blood-boiling conversation than actually doing so. Even if I walk away, I can't deny the feeling of empowerment accompanied by frustration brought about by their misguided judgements. In those instances, I need answers or a defense.

In my twenties, a woman I worked with ignorantly determined my child-free decision was based on my lifestyle choices. She lectured me on the areas I needed to change for true life fulfillment—which by her standards was being a mother. This wasn't the first time someone judged my reason for not wanting children, but with Karen, she was the first to be intrusively vulgar and seemingly out of touch. These conversations took place everywhere: the hallway, the lab, the lunchroom, work travel, and even in the bathroom. She had no idea of my complexities and created a judgment based on the surface. She only saw the weekend routines of beer pong, nights in the city, and a close group of friends. In her opinion, she was a mature, responsible woman who sacrificed her needs for others while also using her divorce and two children to define her admirable self-image, while I was the opposite.

Big surprise there, right?

In her mind, I drove a nice car (an Acura TSX), lived in an upgraded apartment, and went on vacations that were not "family-oriented," so the money I spent held no real substance. To her, I wasn't able to sacrifice my lifestyle, causing her to label me materialistic and superficial.

She constantly compared our similarities before she had children. "You know it is easy to give up drinking, right? I did. We had similar lifestyles. I loved having a good time with an excellent glass or two of Merlot."

I sat there in anticipation, knowing this conversation was going downhill and sideways fast.

She further enlightened me: "I then found out I was pregnant, and that wine didn't have the same desire or taste anymore. I am now drunk on my baby."

Knowing she wasn't done, I just sat there with one eyebrow raised, trying not to roll my eyes.

"I quit cold turkey, and I have never missed it since. It was easy to give up and helped me realize that I might have been too dependent on the wine. Now my child is dependent on me."

Listening to her comments, I started to feel attacked. It's one thing to be chastised around not having children; it's another to be accused of something you are not.

I defensively and adamantly stated my piece. "I'm not dependent on alcohol. I can give up booze or anything else for something I love."

Karen got under my skin, and this is a prime example of when one should walk away.

I didn't.

I couldn't.

I felt the need to defend myself.

Paralyzed from rage, the only thing I could do was shout. Not that shouting my truth would make a difference. She had a combative answer for everything, and her mind was already convinced.

"You are not like me, and I am not dependent on liquor!" I shouted.

With a quick retort, she replied, "How would you know? You have never tried giving it up."

I was furious at this point, with intense emotions taking over. "I am me! I am a smart person who has strong willpower!"

She looked at me smugly. "Oh, OK. I understand. I just want to reiterate; I too didn't think I had a problem until it was time for me to face reality. And thank God I did."

I tried multiple approaches to convince Karen alcohol was not a factor: somber tones stating the truth, defensive attitudes reiterating facts, even dismissive approaches identifying our differences.

Nothing worked.

At that moment, I felt incredible anger toward this woman. Completely exhausted from defending the truth, I regrettably reverted to lying—a tactic that should never be considered.

"Well, you read me like a book. The truth is my sponsor keeps telling me I should wait for my two-week sobriety chip before I think about becoming pregnant."

She stood there silently looking down at the ground. I immediately felt remorse making light of a serious situation many people face. Unfortunately, my anger overpowered my ability to think clearly and walk away.

I am not proud, just honest.

It is important to remember that views from afar only witness surface, not depth, causing arguments to simply be biased opinions.

Not knowing what she had sacrificed, I tried to stay neutral with my remarks, but I was still annoyed. Here I was trying to be the bigger person, and yet she had put no effort into understanding my sacrifices. She only determined I have none because I am not a parent.

With a calm nature, I said, "I see people every day provide for their children by putting themselves last."

With her hip pushed to the side and arms crossed, she missed my intent and continued the passive-aggressive rant.

"Do you think you could give up your luxuries?" she asked.

Staring at her, I sincerely replied, "If I needed to, yes."

With a look of disbelief, she continued her questioning. "You think you would be able to give up your vacations, your parties, and your car? I don't see that happening. That is *you*."

With a slightly higher tone but not defensive, I decided to make a point. "Those materialistic items don't define me at all. Would you like it if I defined you as a woman who drives a beat-up station wagon?"

Her face turned stern and angry. "I have a child!" she snapped.

"Right, but I am only judging from what I see. The same way you do to me."

Completely missing the point, her defense became louder. "I don't have time to go on vacations for myself or buy a fancy car."

Karen was not listening, and it was apparent her judgments would not change. Understanding this, I took the opportunity to stop the conversation by walking away. Given the circumstances, I wish she could have gone on a vacation or even treated herself to the slightest indulgence. It might have provided some exhilaration, possibly making her less judgmental. Truth be told, she was more upset with her own life and found relief by projecting superficial judgments toward me.

A few months later, she left the company without any warning. I never thought seeing a beat-up station wagon leave a parking lot would make me happy, but it did.

Understanding when and how to walk away is pertinent. The topic of finances proves to be just as frequently essential. Finances are an intricate discussion topic where both parents and I agree costs associated with children are substantial.

On many occasions, people questioned money as a factor in my decision not to have children. Other times, people assume I only want to spend on myself. With either encounter, the answer is no.

Even though it is proven raising a child can be expensive: middle-income parents in the United States will spend, on average, $272,049 per child from birth to the age of eighteen. It did not influence my decision. Not wanting to add anxiety, I feel compelled to mention higher education is not included in that average. Housing, food, and childcare are the largest expenses with healthcare, insurance, and transportation rounding out the sum.[5]

While $272,049 is a significant amount of money, the fear of financial instability was not my argument to remain child-free. Admittedly, it is comforting knowing Jim and I can utilize our finances however we feel. We have a secure savings account for emergency situations, the ability to support family or friends, donate to local charities, and splurge on ourselves when necessary. To book that exquisite vacation, upgrade our house in one shot, or buy that luxury car are an opulence of choices we can have without the pressure to save for a child.

Being just the two of us, our future has been decided, and it is important to live a lifestyle mirroring that. When a person considers this approach materialistic, they fail to understand our overall values.

---

5   Tim Parker, "The Cost of Raising a Child in the United States," *Investopedia* (January 9, 2022): http://www.investopedia.com/articles/personal-finance/090415/cost-raising-child-america.asp.

If the desire were strong enough to become a parent, those luxuries and that type of financial thinking would easily be replaced.

Financial discussions can be dreaded conversations, and in my circumstance, it was the main reason why, early in our relationship, Jim and I fought occasionally.

Being of Gen X, I graduated with a degree in environmental geoscience and a minor in chemistry during a recession, in a geologist field that was not hiring. Even if a job was available, the salary was barely enough to keep one's head above water.

I lived on the East Coast, and the cost of living spiked. My very hardworking, middle-class parents somehow made it seem easy to have the cute house, the family, and a small emergency savings fund. Meanwhile, living paycheck-to-paycheck while hoping to secure a stable job was my year-to-year. I panicked because I couldn't save money, and that sense of security was missing. Of course, when you have panic, unemployment, and low income as the variables in an equation, the constant proves to be fights, stress, and tears.

Even now, being comfortable with money in the bank, I always ask my husband if we are OK. A simple purchase of a shirt has me doubting our overall financial stability. Being patient and understanding of what we endured twenty years ago, Jim is constantly reassuring me. He reminds me of our current working situation and financial status and reiterates the differences between our lifestyle now versus then. I know how fortunate I am to purchase something without it breaking the bank, but in my twenties, our financial instability broke my confidence. To those who experience this struggle with children, more power to you. The overall fear and pressure must be undeniable.

One of our biggest fights has been forever engraved in my mind. We were in our twenties, and Jim was the main person supporting our relationship. We recently moved into our first apartment together, and my job situation was dismal. I was in a call center, scheduling CAT and MRI scans. The pay was limited, but at least there was income. Not only was there stress from finances, but I was also worried about success, from both my parents' point of view and my own. Here I was: a graduate with a science degree wanting to change the world, only to end up feeling hopeless and far away from my goal.

After September 11, 2001, the economy and job market collapsed. I had it much easier than some, but the stress of paying bills, getting a job, and trying to be happy was intense. We were babysitting Dawn's two cats while she and her husband were away. The buildup of stress was about to explode onto Jim. We were discussing bills and items to cut back on. Money was so tight that we needed to pick which utility to pay and which to push off for the month.

I know he felt the stress from the financial aspect, but I felt the stress of being a failure. I was the one with the degree. I was the one who was supposed to get a job right after college and start my life—*our* life.

That was the picture society painted for us: graduate with a college degree and everything will fall into place.

Well, it didn't.

My frustration boiled onto Jim, and I did not handle my anger well then. I ended up throwing a clothes hanger at him while screaming absolute nonsense.

He stood there paralyzed.

I was acting like an enraged monster, lashing out at Jim because the pressure finally boiled over. I took all of it out on him.

He was so frustrated he decided to leave.

Overcome with anger, he kicked a pile of laundry in front of the door down the stairs. Turned out that inside the laundry was a cat hiding from all my screaming.

The laundry hit the bottom of the staircase, and the cat squealed and ran under the sofa.

"Oh, my God!" Jim shouted and ran to the sofa. He checked on the cat, who was more scared than hurt. Jim felt horrible, and his body language changed from angry and tense to sad and slouched.

I didn't care if he was concerned. I was even more enraged from his unintentional action. The nonsense I was spewing became louder.

While checking on the cat, I heard the door slam and saw Jim driving away.

The cat was fine, but I was not.

Jim did not come back that night, and neither one of us called. It was just me alone with my thoughts. And let me tell you, I was in terrible company.

At first, I didn't consider myself to be wrong. Those raw feelings and experiences were not fabricated and felt justified. After the anger and emotion subsided, I was able to see more clearly. Though my stress was warranted, my aggression toward Jim was not. I pushed away the person who provided mental stability in our relationship.

Finally, I realized this was all my fault.

A day passed and we sat down for an exceptionally long conversation. I apologized for my behavior, explained my experience, and recognized the pressure he was under. He appreciated and accepted the apology. Even though he knew I was under stress, being vulnerable and open allowed him to gain more clarity toward what I was experiencing. His anger then shifted to empathy and resolution. We proceeded to compile a financial plan for living paycheck-to-paycheck during this long and extremely stressful time.

If a child were part of that scenario, there is no doubt in my mind the intensity would have been insurmountable.

It's understandable why one would question money as a driver for my decision. The stress of finances is no stranger, and with a child, that impact would be significant. Other times, people like Karen assume I believe money not spent on me is money not well spent. Truth be told, if I only had enough cash to purchase one thing for myself or one item for someone else, someone else would have a new item.

Honestly, it's an awesome feeling when I occasionally spend money on myself. It is a feeling that is OK to admit and should not be used against me. To judge my life only from a materialistic viewpoint demonstrates ignorance that defines who you are, not who I am.

Who I am is a person consistently working hard for

accomplishments. Nothing is ever handed over; instead everything is earned. Between restaurant jobs, call scheduling, and retail, I held a multitude of jobs simply to get by. It wasn't until I was hired at a fragrance manufacturer that my future career path shifted. The lab manager saw the desire in me and walked me through essential tasks not part of my job. This provided the insight, passion, and hope for my professional career that was missing.

The job was a temporary assignment, and I fell in love with the industry. The same lab manager had a connection at a larger fragrance company for an entry-level technician position. This was a professional reach that terrified me. Believing this would be the only connection, I did everything to prepare for that interview. I updated my resume, read chemical books, reread some of my college science notes, shadowed my current colleagues, and memorized every solvent known to man. The determination paid off, and I was offered the job. It didn't pay well, but I had finally found something I was passionate about. Hopelessly looking for a career to complete me, the amount of emptiness and fear I felt was large. Having a child during that time would have been incomprehensible. Besides monetary security, a child requires emotional dedication—something I struggled to provide myself with during this time.

After a few years overflowing with career happiness, I still found myself needing money. The economy was rough, and expenses were not going down. Unfortunately for me, the electric company did not accept happiness as a form of currency. Knowing the importance of balancing passion, self-value, confidence, and salary, I applied for a lab technician position at a food company.

I did not have a background or experience in food science (a job requirement), but I applied the same confidence, risk, work ethic, and knowledge to getting the job. That determination provided me with the position at Cadbury Adams, which changed my life. Though a lower title position, it provided a significant salary increase, benefits, and career growth. The Cadbury work family instilled values, openness, and a general sense of worth, which molded me into the boss lady I am today. They believed in me, and I was able to prove myself by growing from a lab technician to a scientist within my eight-year career.

Ten years in the making, Jim and I finally felt comfortable with both our careers and finances. We planned a wedding, moved into a more stable apartment, and invested in our savings.

In our early thirties, we capitalized on new advancements and moved to Wisconsin. We were able to save money, buy a house, and take that next leap in adulting.

Six years after living in Wisconsin, Jim and I needed to move back to the tristate New England area in Massachusetts. The expensive cost of living pressed our confidence three months in when Jim was suddenly let go from his job of over ten years.

Fifteen years later, back in Massachusetts, we lived on one salary; however, this time my husband was unhappy. The unhappy part was what hurt me most. He wanted to pursue a different career and obtain a degree. We reviewed our finances and decided Jim was going back to school. This was now my chance to thank him for all the mental, physical, and financial support throughout the years. Twenty years ago, the thought of me supporting our family was unimaginable, and though we are in a more stable stage in our lives, he has managed his stress much better than I have.

Not one hanger has flown in my direction, and I can assure you all cats are safe.

To a certain extent, I understand how it feels when things are not viable. I've sacrificed and worked hard to get to this point. There are luxuries I've purchased to remind me of my journey, such as my Audi (a car I've always wanted and never thought was attainable). Again, for those who do judge my lifestyle to be materialistic, may I remind some of you that your choice to have children allows you to drive that sick minivan with the televisions on the back seats, something my car does not have.

When discussing topics like children, it is more about explaining a point of view while listening to someone else's. I understand I'm not going to change the mind of a mother of five about having children, and she is not going to change mine. Which brings me to Susan.

Through a mutual acquaintance, I had a conversation at a restaurant with Susan—a young, stay-at-home mother of three. With a single-family income, her husband supports them by working in construction. Susan continuously discussed her family, including her parents who lived next door and babysat on the weekdays.

Sincerely happy for her loving and close family, I emphasized how lucky she must feel. "It's really nice and convenient having your parents so close. They can support you when you need it."

Susan's face went from a smile to an instant glare.

"Do you have children?" she asked aggressively.

Knowing this discussion was about to take a drastic turn, I quickly responded, "No, I don't."

With an even faster reply and a defensive tone, she said, "Then you have no right to speak on a topic you know nothing about!"

I was confused over her reaction and presumed the shift was due to the word "convenient." Maybe she took it out of context and assumed I was judging her in a negative way. Knowing how it feels to be judged, I wanted to quickly clear the air. Sadly, I wasn't given the moment to ask or apologize. Something switched on in Susan, and she went off on a tirade. She got up from the table, walked up and down the bar aisle, and spewed harsh judgements toward me.

"This snobby, superficial bitch thinks she can judge me. Well, the only one who matters is God, and he is judging you right now!" she exclaimed while pointing at me.

She continued with even more screaming: "You will be alone. That is what you deserve!"

I kid you not: after twenty minutes of this, the people in the restaurant ignored her. They went about their day, watching television, continuing their own conversations, and eating food. I sat there feeling sorry and sad. Not for myself but for her.

With a flustered face, she walked to the door, still pointing that index finger toward me. "I hope you enjoy your fancy life, eating your precious sushi and relaxing in your hot tub!"

Blank stare and confusion. That was all I had going on.

I was so confused and utterly shocked by her behavior that I just couldn't respond. It was probably better off that way. Trying to calmly establish a point of view during an instance like that is usually impossible. Staying quiet and allowing Susan to express herself was the best course. Clearly this anger was not only toward me. Her life had more complexities in it than what was being portrayed, and if I'm advocating for people to not surface judge me, then I must remember to do the same. Honestly, this scenario is similar to the hanger-throwing, accidental cat-tossing fight with Jim. It was only a matter of time before life's pressures exploded. Unfortunately, he was in my crossfire at the time, and I was in hers. With that said, no one deserves to be belittled or screamed at, no matter what circumstance someone is experiencing. Especially when intentions are pure, not malicious.

The Dalai Lama once said, "Don't let the behavior of others destroy your inner peace."[6]

On that day, I was even more confident in who I am and proud of the decisions I've made. Susan from Wisconsin (you know who you are), if by some weird chance you read this, I wish you the best. I also want you to know that I don't like sushi, I haven't been in a hot tub in over ten years, and I'm fabulous.

---

6   Dalai Lama, "How to See Yourself As You Really Are," *Atria* (2007), reprint edition.

Chapter 4
FEMININITY

"Can you feel feminine without having a child?"

Mona Lisa Vito from *My Cousin Vinny* said it best: "My biological clock is (*taps her foot*) TICKING LIKE THIS, and the way this case is going, I ain't never getting married!"[1] This line sounds all too familiar. Not because I say this every day, but because others swear my biological clock will force my nay-baby mind to make a yay-baby decision.

Is there such a thing as a biological clock? If so, are its powers strong enough to change the mind of a determined, independent and defined woman? The science nerd in me will tell you cells, tissues, and organs have some type of internal clock that senses light, darkness, and other rhythmic cycles that are coordinated by your brain. The most commonly referenced biological clock—human fertility—is both scientifically accurate and mentally persuading.

Fertility for women declines around their mid-thirties. The mental pressure from the metaphoric biological clock ticking down holds a significant grip. Even men experience the countdown. Though not commonly recognized, since the stigma is attached to women, men

---

1   *My Cousin Vinny*, Jonathan Lynn: director, 1992.

can also attribute pressure from their own version of a biological clock. A man in his seventies can get a woman pregnant, and at that age, the alarm clock of fear is wondering how much time is left. Is there enough time to be the father he wants to be? Does he have enough lifespan to instill traditions and family legacies he has experienced? Can he even bend over to pick up the child from the ground? These heavy loads for both men and women have the weight of a ticking time bomb. I am lucky enough to have never experienced a detonation. Instead, my countdowns are solely used to celebrate each new year with gratitude.

I never felt that urgency, trusted alarm, or even the ticking of a clock indicating the necessity for a child. When I was in my twenties, many people waived off my intent, stating I was young, followed by their reassured permission that I should find myself first.

When I was in my early thirties, I was told there was still time to decide to have a child. Apparently, the clock does not truly begin until you find yourself at the age of researching anti-aging face creams.

By the time I got to my late thirties, I stopped hearing the rebuttals and was littered with compliments like, "You're a great person," "You are so smart," and "You're beautiful," with the hopes to convince me to have a baby before it was too late.

I must admit, it was a genius tactic.

Who doesn't want to hear positive attributes about themselves?

Now that I am in my forties, many people discuss the great medical advancements, which result in healthier geriatric pregnancies and babies. In vitro fertilization, oocyte cryopreservation, prenatal supplements, technology, and diets have evolved, supporting increased birth rates over the age of forty. Even with these progressions, geriatric pregnancy continues to hold higher medical risks for both the carrier and baby. Gestational diabetes, high blood pressure, preeclampsia, higher birth weight, placenta previa, miscarriage, and Down syndrome are just a few risks associated with a pregnancy later in life.[2] Not to focus only on the

---

2   Alesandra Benisek, "Pregnant at 40: What to Expect," *WebMD*, April 12, 2022: https://www.webmd.com/baby/pregnant-at-40.

negative, it can be argued that having a child past your "youthful" years provides benefits as well. One might be more financially stable, mature, or professionally committed, alleviating those stress factors in life.

No matter the advancements in science, my status in life, or my supposed internal notifier, for the last twenty-four years and counting, no alarm has gone off, and I've never had to convince my mind or heart to think differently. Despite what some might believe, this feeling doesn't make me naïve or cold-hearted, nor does it make me ignorant of what others might experience. It simply means I have thought long and hard about this milestone. I have not wavered on these thoughts or feelings, and I took a different journey than others.

Once again, that is OK.

Recently, I was standing in a makeup aisle at a department store, and a woman asked me what type of perfume I was wearing. After I told her, we started to chat about all the different concealers and started reviewing the best one for dark eye circles.

"I need a great eye concealer. I am tired all the time," the woman said. She then proceeded to discuss how her young children are constantly keeping her up.

"Do you have children?" she asked.

"No," I said.

"That's OK. You still have plenty of time!" she informed me.

"How old do you think I am?" I asked out of curiosity.

"Early to mid-thirties," she stated without hesitation.

First off, thank you! I will hold that little nugget of confidence for a future pick me up!

Though still wanting to bask in the compliment, I knew I should correct her. "Thanks, but I am actually forty-one."

"Oh . . ." she said awkwardly after a pause with no eye contact.

I assumed her awkwardness was because of my age and its association with pregnancy, so to break the tension, I decided to be more open and mention my decision. "I chose not to have kids. My husband and I don't want children."

Instantly, the woman looked up, and her demeanor changed.

"You know, if you change your mind, there are some great advancements with older women and healthier pregnancies," she enthusiastically declared. "There is still time and hope. My cousin waited until she was forty."

Now, being in my forties, I have heard the term "medical advancements" more times than I can count. A simple "thank you" is how I've been responding to the sea of people who have miraculously become reproductive endocrinologists overnight.

Without a biological clock constantly going off, does that make me less of a woman?

With my discussions, I have always argued "no." I feel feminine despite not having or wanting children. I am a woman because I am strong enough to admit that. Surprisingly, there are people who view this differently. To them, a woman revolves around children in some capacity. From the physical nature of pregnancy and childbirth to the nurturing aspects of being a mother, a child must be involved to fulfill that definition.

At yet another fun-filled corporate family picnic, I was staffing a bowling activity when a coworker introduced me to her grandmother. Since there were many children at my activity, the grandmother pleasantly started up a conversation about children.

"Do you have any children?" she warmly asked.

If I had a dollar for every time someone asked me this, I'd be a billionaire.

I quickly responded "No" with a small grin and a confident head shake.

Swiftly moving her hand over her heart, she sincerely detailed: "You are missing out on one of the greatest gifts a woman can experience. Life's biggest privilege when being a woman is to be associated as a mother."

Not that this grandmother was rude or pushy; I just simply wasn't looking for an in-depth child-centered conversation.

I was more focused on when Bingo was starting.

In an attempt to continue the conversation, I replied, "The whole process of pregnancy is something I marvel at. What the body can do is amazing."

Not realizing the caliber of my statements, I quickly noticed she was aggressively nodding in agreement. "Right, and you are not taking advantage of your God-given right. Women need to understand their role, which is to bear children. This is our responsibility. The men are to support us, and we need to support the child," she said.

It was clear this woman's point of view is considered old school: a woman in the house, raising the children, while the man is out supporting the family at work.

Understanding where she was coming from, I wanted to emphasize my stance. "I personally don't believe it is necessary for me to have a child just because I can."

"Can you feel like a woman, knowing this?" she empathetically questioned.

In my life, many versions of this question have been asked, sometimes with disgust, other times with chastisement. This woman's tone suggested empathy combined with genuine curiosity and concern. I felt honored to explain my viewpoint to her because she was listening, invested, and humble.

"Sure, you can. You relate it to your own perspective," I explained.

For me, my perspective reflects a certain type of personality and attitude—being an open-minded, self-aware, and strongly independent person who lives each day with integrity and values. Though opposite to her catered perspective, this sustains my lifestyle.

We talked for a while, and though I can't recall the additional conversations we had after, I do remember feeling heard. She wasn't judgmental or defensive but instead took the time to understand where I was coming from and listened to my choice. What started off as a Bingo distraction ended up being one of the best moments I've ever had on this subject.

Could I feel more feminine if I had a child? Maybe. I don't know.

Sometimes people describe femininity as that "mothering nature." I know I am not a mother, but I demonstrate fostering attributes: ensuring those around me are happy, healthy, comfortable, and safe (not to mention well-fed—remember, I'm half Italian. It is in my blood to be a proper host and prepare a meal that can feed an army).

Truth of the matter, gender reflection and roles are pivoting as are the expectations of how one should feel. Gender is being addressed as something more than what the past has dictated.

The Confidence Code, a New York Times Best Seller by Katty Kay and Claire Shipman, addresses topics such as the misunderstood quality of confidence in women. Is confidence something only a select few have? Can you learn confidence? Why do women—even successful women—struggle with feelings of self-doubt? Is it from influence or is it from our DNA makeup? Could it be both?[3]

These journalists investigate areas of neuroscience, psychology, and female leadership in politics, arts, sports, and the military to identify how female leaders take action in life. Uncovering that confidence is partly influenced by genetics, but it is not fixed.

Take a page from some inspirational childless women like devoted civil rights activist Susan B. Anthony, Mexican painter Frida Kahlo, US Supreme Court judge Sonia Sotomayor, author Jane Austen, and the American Media mogul Oprah Winfrey. Not only did these women succeed beyond the limits of their fields, but they also pivoted outside the social norm and chose to take on more action related to themselves.

When individually dictating the ideals for life—especially the preference for children—religion, ethnicity, and media are strong influential factors. For example, in ethnically Chinese populations around the world, birth rates spike in lucky Zodiac years, like the year of the Dragon. Similarly, when growing up in an environment surrounded by extended family or a religious community, fertility encouragement

---

3   Claire Shipman and Katty Kay, *The Confidence Code* (Harper Business, 2014).

grows. Meanwhile, access to modern mass media coverage such as the reality television show *16 and Pregnant* or even Brazilian soap operas have caused decreased desires for having a child.[4]

If you believe that you are not destined to have a child, then you must own that. Dare yourself to be authentic enough to represent women and be classified as feminine, all without having a child. Challenge the system, advocate for your risks, and undo what has been physically wired in both your mind and society's perspective.

If all else fails, ask yourself, "What would Oprah Winfrey do?"

I am surprised by the large number of people who genuinely believe a woman is defined by reproduction. What's even more astonishing are the levels associated with this. A small handful of my encounters described the act of adoption or the inability to bear children as less feminine, highlighting these ideologies exist.

More compassionate beliefs revolve around God's decision. With sympathy, people explained infertility as God's decision. With God having other plans in store for those particular individuals, the woman, who is still considered feminine, is not at fault for missing out on what they consider the greatest gift in life.

Once at a wedding, I was relaxing at a table with a religious family friend after dancing the night away. Children were devouring the desserts, and the atmosphere was celebratory, but sometimes joyous occasions like this one bring up stark reminders or painful scenarios.

With all the kids at the wedding, this particular family friend was somber. I couldn't understand why she was not happy during such a joyous occasion. Out of regard, I asked her if she was OK. At first, she brushed off her look of despair by stating she was zoning out, but I felt that wasn't the truth. Not wanting to press her, I respected her boundaries. It was only when a few kids started to dance in a group in front of our table when she opened up about children. I didn't even

---

4   Lyman Stone, "What Makes People Have Babies: The Link Between Cultural Values and Fertility Rates" *Public Discourse*, May 7, 2019, https://www.thepublicdiscourse.com/2019/05/51661/.

need to ask her about it; instead she told me the "zoning out" was her contemplating a reality without children. The look of sadness on her face would make you think she was going through infertility at that very moment. The mere thought of not being able to have that "gift from God" was devastating to her.

Because she was so open with me, I felt comfortable enough to ask her about adoption. In my mind, I was curious if adoption would be a consideration given her love and desire for a child—or if it was a biological must. I have read blogs and listened to stories where people worried their connection—both physically and mentally—to a child through adoption or even surrogacy could be limited compared to a biological birth. Feeling how important a child was to her, I wanted to know if the potential distress of adoption would deter her from becoming a mother.

Her answer was mesmerizing.

"I would consider adoption," she said sadly while looking down.

I knew there was more to her answer. I sensed she didn't mind adoption, but something was off.

She looked up. "My parents wouldn't be happy. To them, it isn't God's plan."

I sat there heartbroken for her, carrying this stress based on a moment that is supposed to be wonderful. I didn't say a word. I just sympathetically stared at her.

"If I need to adopt, I must get permission from the church, which can be denied. I also must allow my husband the opportunity to find a woman who is fertile and can carry out his legacy," she sorrowfully said.

Heart-wrenching.

I was under the impression that a mother, no matter if the baby came from her body, a baby-momma, or a stranger, would be considered a woman. After listening to these encounters, I knew that is not the case.

Other views around children are also divided.

When I was visiting a production site in Arkansas for work, I saw an event happening at a park by my hotel. Thinking it was a food festival, I went to check it out. I mean, who wouldn't want a fried Oreo and a soft pretzel on a summer night?

There was a stage, music, food, and a lot of people. What I walked myself into, without knowing, was an antiabortion rally.

I froze.

Standing in the middle of this field with a soft pretzel in my hand, I didn't know what to do. All I kept thinking was to find the closest exit. I did not want to engage in this topic. Not because I wouldn't talk to this group or respect their thoughts, I just sensed I was the only person there with different beliefs.

As I walked toward the exit, protesters chanted. I weaved in and out of conversations taking place, and the base of the music became louder.

"Motherhood begins with conception!"

"Murder is abortion!"

"Murder is miscarriage!"

"Mothers should sacrifice their lives for their children's lives!"

This was intense. No pretzel was worth this kind of assault. I did not agree with what they were saying and simply needed to leave without causing a disturbance. This instance—allowing others to demonstrate their own beliefs—highlights how easily a topic such as motherhood can invite completely different views.

Even though some of my encounters have been difficult, I've loved most of my discussions about my child-free ways. Many people have been forthcoming with both positive and negative experiences. In my own bubble, I assumed the judgement stopped if you had a child. It turns out, there are granular debates parents go through with other parents, society, and even themselves.

A significant disagreement in the parenting world that has been brought to my attention is breast milk versus formula. According to some mothers, if you don't breastfeed, you are providing a manufactured formula deprived of key nutrients, which will stunt the growth and development of your child. Additionally, some argue bottle-feeding is a "lazy" form of parenting.

What? Even *I* know there is nothing lazy about raising a child.

Hearing parents put down other parents is very distressing. Candidly, it is another example of how society is generally failing. You breastfeed your child, but the other mom doesn't? I still don't understand how that puts your child at an advantage. If it did, why condemn?

Working in the food industry, I can confirm that formulations must follow significant guidelines before manufacturing to ensure they meet health, nutrition, and other regulations. The formulation may not mirror all the nutrients from breast milk, but it isn't poison. Instead, the crudeness delivered by those who are inconsiderate is the toxin.

Being a woman is hard enough, and adding motherhood is another layer of complexity. There is never an adequate time to bring someone down; instead we all should be lifting each other up. As I think about my journey without kids, I know I will get asked questions no matter if I am younger or older. The judgment, conversations, and explanations won't stop, but I can simply walk away. However, a mother will need to be involved in groups associated with her children twenty-four seven. For me, this is a grass is greener scenario. My side of the fence is safer and greener. So, to all the moms out there who occasionally need to jump over the fence, my side will welcome you and your children.

Though, fair warning, when you jump to my side of the fence, the clear liquid in my bottle may not be water, the gummy bears have rum in them, and consult me first if your kid wants to eat a brownie.

Besides the biological clock, does physical appearance support femininity? There have been societal movements and advancements shifting the typical feminine-defined look. Unfortunately, there is still a long way to travel to get outside the stereotypical, female path of long hair, perky breasts, curves, and petite features.

Unladylike: A Field Guide to Smashing the Patriarchy and Claiming Your Space, by Cristen Conger and Caroline Ervin, explores what patriarchy looks like in the real world by laying out double standards, discussing astounding women in history, and social justice principles. *Unladylike* emphasizes that no matter who we are or what we look like, we are not impervious to the effects of patriarchy—from entitlement for a man to objectification of a woman or dehumanization of a nonbinary.[5]

Jim and I are members of a country club where we frequently enjoy the atmosphere, food, and drinks, along with playing many rounds of golf, pickleball, and tennis. Sitting at the club house waiting for my husband's round of golf to end, I experienced a great example of stereotypical behavior. A group of older gentlemen were relaxing at a table in front of me. I had my sunglasses on and was pretending to read, and the men were apparently unaware I was able to hear their conversation.

One man nudged his head toward me. "That brunette has an athletic build and should have a powerful swing on the course." He then went on to detail his surprise when a petite blonde woman showed a powerful drive. He repeatedly exclaimed his amazement with the "small-framed, good-looking woman's course dominance."

I sat at the table wondering why the man described this woman the way he did. Why has society created expectations around someone's specific looks? And why does her hair color even matter?

What it really boils down to is this: words are powerful, but the unconscious bias is even more so.

The judgments, however, are never-ending with gender bias. A woman who tirelessly defends a strong decision she believes in is feisty, but if she were a man, he would be determined. Skillful reasoning and persuasion from a woman is pushy, but if a man does it, he is persuasive. My personal favorite, though, is that when a woman takes charge, she's bossy, but when a man does so, he's driven. One thing I do know is whether you call me feisty, determined, pushy, persuasive, bossy, or driven, I will be confidently genuine.

---

5   Cristen Conger and Caroline Ervin, *Unlady Like: A Field Guide to Smashing the Patriarchy and Claiming Your Space* (Ten Speed Press, 2018).

When certain groups of people view me as being less of a woman for not having a child, they are the ones instilling negative bias. In a lot of instances, you can express your opinion, and I will respect that. But to blatantly state I am not feminine because I decided to not have children is flat out ignorant. In a reverse action, I could state conforming to social norms and expectations, though powerful influences of behavior, are classic excuses for your presence.

My overall idea of femininity would be a passionate, independent person who is mentally strong, capable of success, and confident in oneself—indicating the ability to shine in all sizes, shapes, colors, and attitudes. A lot of the world needs to realize this. We also need to realize how society notoriously stops at the surface and compiles an opinion. In return, we must require more patience and educate one another. Through my encounters, my overall realization proves judgements do not define the person being judged; rather they define the person who is judging.

Chapter 5
SELFISHNESS

"Can you not give up your lifestyle?

Survival of the fittest is a powerful justification for selfish behavior. Originating from Darwin's natural selection, those capable of "looking out for number one," in a biological sense, would survive, while natural selection would eliminate those less equipped. The reasons why and how selfishness occurs are commonly debated between human hardwiring and sociocultural influences. Understandably, it's a sensitive matter when someone's definition of selfishness contradicts your own. Is it selfish of a person eating their raspberry chicken vinaigrette salad to not think about the farmer who endured the grueling early morning labor for their delicious meal? Or is it selfish of the billionaire entrepreneur to donate only to charities and communities close to their mission and values? Where does that line cross, and who decided that threshold? Personally, I would define selfishness as thinking exclusively with oneself in mind, concentrating on one's own advantage and deliberately ignoring consequences or regard for others.

Taking my definition of selfishness into consideration, imagine being constantly defined as selfish for not having or wanting a child—a personal decision that took cautious, emotional, and calculated conversations and considerations. Not to mention it has zero effect on the majority of the people accusing me.

Since deciding to not have children, this large pill to swallow has been a constant prescription in my life. Though this judgement has slowed down in my forties, I can't see it completely disappearing, maybe just becoming a lower dosage.

What is intriguing, though, are the beliefs behind individual perceptions of selfishness. Some of the most interesting conversations I've had revolved around a plane's emergency oxygen mask. You've heard these instructions before: Pull the mask toward you, place the mask over your nose and mouth, and breathe in.

Place your mask on first before helping others.

The specific instructions dictating the correct usage of the oxygen mask is not the issue at hand. Instead, supporting yourself first before helping others forces the conundrum within some people.

In the prototype lab at work, a coworker and I were discussing NFL quarterback Tom Brady and his apparent GOAT (Greatest of All Time) status.

Don't get me started on that!

Our conversation shifted to Tom's disciplined eating habits, which were influenced by his then supermodel wife, Gisele Bündchen. From there we started talking about her beauty and her love for her family, country, and the environment. Transitioning into different topics, I brought up an article that essentially labeled her selfish. Summarizing the context: Gisele described the need for moms to put themselves first and referenced the oxygen mask analogy as support.[1] This comment created some media and social backlash, labeling and judging the supermodel mom as being selfish, while others viewed her as truthful.

"I agree wholeheartedly with Gisele's comments," I said.

---

1   Kate Winter, "Supermodel Gisele Bundchen says mothers should put themselves first in order to be a good parent," *Daily Mail*, October 21, 2014, https://www.dailymail.co.uk/femail/article-2801325/supermodel-gisele-bundchen-says-mothers-order-good-parent.html.

"No way. Purely selfish," my coworker declared.

At first, I thought she was disagreeing with Gisele's comment because of her status in society, but that wasn't the case. She simply viewed her as a terrible mother because she followed the "put your mask on first" step.

"How selfish can one be when they would rather see their child suffer than themselves?" she asked with an aggressive tone.

I just sat there and listened.

Quickly pacing back and forth, she exclaimed, "I would much rather take the chance and die first than not protect my children!"

I knew this coworker was animated and very distressed by the scenario, yet I felt the need to reiterate my opinion.

"Like I said before, I agree with Gisele's logic."

I was quickly dismissed.

"You don't have kids. You have no idea the impact this statement has," she quickly said.

Biting my tongue, I needed to collect my thoughts. I calmly took a breath.

"Right, I don't have children, but I do have family and friends. What if I was on the plane with my mother who barely flies or my nephews who are autistic? They are not my children, but they are part of my soul, and I would still place my mask on first," I explained.

Without missing a second, she responded, "It's not the same scenario."

Feeling her tense response, I knew there was nothing I could say that would change her mind. Instead, any opposing thoughts or facts that went against her belief would cause more negative backlash.

It was time to walk away.

While walking away, I started to slightly open my thought process. Knowing myself and always thinking of others, if the airline industry did not explain the necessity to place my mask on first, I probably wouldn't. In a way, I understand her angle. With that said, all airline industries provide the same valid oxygen mask instruction to provide key responsibilities that will reduce confusion and increase coherence during an emergency. Hypoxia or hypoxemia, low oxygen in your tissues or blood, are dangerous conditions that can affect your organs in minutes.[2]

Planes are pressurized to support those necessary oxygen levels. Above ten thousand feet, the amount of oxygen in the blood begins to decrease, and by twenty thousand feet, the concentration of oxygen in the blood is only 65 percent saturation. At these levels, normal human functions like cognitive thinking and consciousness are interrupted. If an emergency were to occur requiring oxygen in the plane, an individual's time of useful response or consciousness is limited. Around thirty-five thousand feet, which is the typical flying altitude, response timing for rational action may only be fifteen seconds, justifying the need to support oneself first.[3]

Although scientifically proven to save both you and your loved one's lives, many people still indicate they would disregard the rule to help their loved ones, no matter the consequence.

Who knew turbulence can happen both in the air and on the ground?

Did you also know you don't need to give up your lifestyle to have children? Judging by the large number of people who've said this to me, one would assume this is true.

A friend of mine who never intended to have children but was blessed with two was adamant about her dominating lifestyle balance: soccer mom by day while still enjoying all her favorite activities like book club, shopping, yoga, and date nights.

After successfully getting the kids to bed or tending to all their needs, I don't doubt it's possible for a parent to curl up with a favorite blanket, a glass of merlot, a good book, or even go out on the town. Even though I don't have children, I am not oblivious to those who do. My family and friends with children partake in some well-deserved,

2   Carol DerSarkissian, MD, "Hypoxia and Hypoxemia," August 10, 2022, https://www.webmd.com/asthma/guide/hypoxia-hypoxemia.

3   "Hypoxia," *SkyBRARY*, https://skybrary.aero/articles/hypoxia.

child-free moments. Those same friends have openly stated their life and lifestyle changed the moment they had children. No more spontaneous trips. No more late nights out or sleep in the mornings. No more focus on two but instead a party of three. Actually, their focus and worry go straight to the kid while everything else takes a back seat. So, we can all argue until we're milk drunk, but the truth is, you absolutely give up some of your former self when you have children—and that is OK.

For me, that reality of sacrifice is a large enough reason to not have children. And to be clear, that is not being selfish but honest and self-aware.

My lifestyle has changed and evolved throughout the years. In my twenties, I was all about the quantity of friends. It just so happened I met some of the most important people then— equating quantity to quality. The twenties were about establishing myself in my inner circles, figuring out my career path, and learning how to survive adulting.

Jim and I started to build the fundamentals necessary to live together. Sure, I targeted the typical design aspects but more importantly the overall feel. I wanted the environment to be inviting, not just for our friends and family but also for both our opinions, disagreements, expectations, and memories. Being as stressed as we were due to finances and career opportunities, I knew in our small one-bedroom apartment that there needed to be a place where we could individually express ourselves and be alone if necessary.

During this time, it was difficult figuring out who I wanted to be professionally, but ensuring that Jim and I understood the necessity of our own space and alone time was easy. Establishing that provided foundation allowed us to be individuals while being a couple.

In my early thirties I focused on job satisfaction, shelter, and responsibilities. During this period, I clawed my way to establish a career through constant hard work, long hours, classes, promotions, and knowledge growth, resulting in a better salary and apartment living for Jim and me. We started developing an adequate life that didn't focus on the day-to-day but was more future centric.

Upon seeing progression with my career and finances, I pushed for a greater social life in my late thirties. Jim and I explored different cities, vacationed as much as possible, moved to a new state, and celebrated life with that same inner circle of friends from our twenties, as well as the new group we'd formed throughout the years.

Now in my early forties, I take the path of being perfectly imperfect with level-headed goals set to accomplish. Being more tenured and established, Jim's and my needs have taken priority, and this lifestyle is not worth giving up. My journey is a continuous evolution, and I'm content. Jim and I still have that special place for individuality in our home and life. Financially, we are stable, and the expectations I set for myself are realistically manageable.

It's normal and natural to change, and I can adapt. My lifestyle is not always about me. Parents have the responsibility to think of their kids first, which establishes a good moral foundation. With some situations, people fail to realize a person without a child also has that responsible moral foundation. This constant scrutiny is difficult to experience, especially when it isn't valid. Every decision I make, no matter the multitude, I take Jim into consideration. How will this affect him? How will he feel about this? When is the right time to engage in his opinion? All these questions, emotions, and thoughts come into my mind before I process how it affects me.

I had a significant opportunity to work abroad for a short-term assignment. Before I could even say I was interested (which I was), I needed to know Jim's opinion. Does he think this is safe? Does he believe this is a good career opportunity? Does he even know how to turn on the stove, or will he be eating take out for the next six months?

I didn't know.

What I did know was the significance of this career move. If he believed I shouldn't go, I would listen and understand his reasoning and have more detailed conversations before *we* decided. Why? Because he is more significant in my life than my thoughts or wants alone. And let me tell you, if Jim were opposed to this situation and discussed steadfast and passionate reasonings, my decision would have been not to go—a decision that would have been difficult but necessary since we're a team, a team that together decided to not have children. I don't know about you, but to me this sounds exactly like what a "selfish person" would do!

One evening when I was in a crowded restaurant, two women were out to dinner with very rambunctious children. The kids were running around the dining room, rolling on the ground, and screaming at one another. Assuming these two women were the children's mothers, they did an excellent job ignoring the situation happening around them. They simply sipped on their drinks and had a conversation while their tiny tornadoes were mentally and physically destroying the environment. Halfway through their conversation, I thought these women sensed stares from the dining room. They stopped speaking with each other and looked over at me. Believing they acknowledged the chaos, I just smiled, reassuring them their kids were not bothering me.

Quickly after my thoughtful gesture, the women started talking about me.

"It must be nice to be by yourself," one woman condescendingly said to her friend.

With a defeated and tired tone, the other woman replied, "My 'me days' are over."

I understand these comments are general statements, but that moment made me stop and think. From the very beginning of my meal, I had been inconvenienced by their uncontrollable children. Putting myself in their shoes, I sympathized and showed signs of empathy while trying to ignore the disarray around me. I received no acknowledgment of my gesture or an apology for their children's behavior but instead more "woe is me" and overall judgements. I believe their feelings were valid, but why am I the one always trying on the shoes? When will someone try on my size six-and-a-half flats?

Why was I alone? Was it by choice? If so, how can these women confidently determine this was positive? Was it because their current situation seemed more extreme? Sure, on the surface, my dinner was less complicated, but who knew within? This is where thinking of others before judgment is essential. I could have been stood-up. I could have been depressed or even lonely. Either way, there were many possible explanations as to why I was by myself, but those women didn't care, because table five's life seemed easier than theirs.

Wanting an easier life, a specific lifestyle, or not wanting change are key assumptions people make based on my child-free decision. I'm also reminded by women closer to my age that professional sacrifices and motherhood are becoming less of an issue in today's society. Though I appreciate the reminder and the encouragement for women, I do see this balance and powerful message everywhere. More companies understand the fundamental need for an environment where professional growth and personal work-life balance are the principal culture. Still, if I were to look back to the early seventies, eighties, and nineties, that positive encouragement was not the approach.

Growing up during those times, the rise of women from household to the professional executive suite was a slow uphill battle. Some people allowed that reality to influence their family decisions. For me, since I knew I did not want children, this circumstance was not a factor. Since I chose to not be a mom, I could focus on my career without the worry of balancing motherhood.

Take the movie *Baby Mama* with Tina Fey and Amy Poehler.[4] The opening monologue talks about Tina Fey's character, a highly successful VP who did everything correct to achieve the youngest VP title at her company. She didn't cry at meetings, wore the right clothing, said all the right things, and put up with weird upper-management guys, only to end up being the oldest mom at preschool. While acknowledging how unfair her choice was, she noted some women get pregnant, and she got promotions.

That movie came out in 2008. Let that sink in.

4   *Baby Mama*, Michael McCullers: director, 2008.

Throughout my career I've been lucky enough to travel all over the world and engage myself with other cultures and environments, giving me quite the detailed résumé. I generated so many memories and made some amazing global friends. Without my career, I know some of my adventures would never have become a reality. I also know that if I had a child, taking those adventures would have been a much harder decision to make (probably resulting in missed opportunities and no passport stamps). But again, this wasn't a reason for me not to have children.

In my late teens and early twenties, I never thought I would go to Thailand or live in South Africa. Traveling wasn't a personal or professional aspiration, but because of those exposures, my fortunate life has been molded and enriched with cultural opportunities I am grateful for.

I am also grateful for my authenticity and transparent personality. When people assume I don't like children, they are taken back by my direct answer. I love children, but I love myself more.

By understanding the impact and weight kids would have on my life, I bravely identify my happiness as being more important. This innocent statement demonstrates the love I have for myself. It is not selfish or shameful to admit self-worth, even if it goes against a societal norm. We need to celebrate and acknowledge this more, rather than chastise others for doing so.

Talking to a group of mothers at (another) child's birthday party, I was cautiously asked a few questions about my no-baby journey.

"You must like kids," one mother stated.

"I do," I quickly responded.

Kids are funny, smart, and intriguing. Not to mention they say the darndest, unfiltered things!

At this birthday party, I played with all the kiddos, and they gravitated toward me. I played hide-and-seek with a bunch of eight-year-olds while holding a two-year-old who never left my side, was invited to not one but *three* princess tea parties and an all-boys GI Joe club, was escorted to the cool kids table to eat and feed children that I had met an hour prior, maneuvered my adult body through the kids' jungle gym while getting passed multiple times on the monkey bars, and heard several children ask their parents if I could come over to play and babysit in the future.

I was and still am the cool aunt, and I enjoy every minute of it.

I also enjoy the satisfaction of handing those children back to their parents.

"You're so good with children. Why did you decide not to have them?" another woman asked.

"I like kids, but I love me more," I truthfully stated.

I'm usually a little apprehensive after I provide this reason since reactions can vary. Some people are offended and walk away, which two people did from that birthday circle. Other times, people explain why my belief is wrong and boldly judge me based on that comment alone. Be that as it may, there are plenty of times people will surprise you with support and praise.

One woman who walked away came back to the circle. She handed me a juice box and raised hers in the air.

"Cheers to all the women who are strong and proud!" she said.

"CHEERS!" we all exclaimed.

At that very moment, Mott's apple juice never tasted so good.

Don't get me wrong; not all moments result in a toast to my profound identity.

At a large popular beer festival, I was having an enjoyable day trying local brews, hanging out with my friends, and soaking in the fun outdoor atmosphere. I was waiting in line for an alcoholic refreshment and found myself standing next to a woman by herself holding a similar stein. With sunglasses on and a constant smile on her face, she looked approachable, friendly, and happy to be there.

While waiting in line, she turned to me and said, "I am lucky I found a babysitter today! My normal one was sick. My husband and I didn't want to miss this event."

"I can imagine," I replied.

"Oh, you have kids?" she questioned.

"No. No children for me," I answered.

"Children not in the cards for you?" she asked, staring at me with a smile on her face.

"Actually, no. My husband and I don't want children," I confidently said.

"Hmm. How come you don't want children?" she blatantly asked.

With her upfront personality, I assumed it was safe for me to match that intensity.

"Because I love myself more than the idea of having a child," I stated.

I was wrong; that intensity was not meant to be matched.

It was not safe.

"Are you serious? That is the most egotistical, self-centered thing I have ever heard. What kind of woman are you? You are a snob."

Slightly dazed by her reaction, I sat there collecting my thoughts and trying to decide if I should walk away. Spoiler alert: I didn't walk away. I had devoted too much time to this particular beer line and was not about to walk away from this stein. Instead, I reminded myself to stay calm and respond with the basics.

"It is important to know who you are and what you want out of life."

"Oh, please, that is what selfish people say," she responded.

"OK, that's fine," I answered.

During that moment I could have continued explaining, but why bother? Why do I care about a stranger's opinion when I would never go to them for advice? Or better yet, pick them out from a crowd of people? This woman definitely did not appreciate my decision, and that's OK. The opinion I have of myself and the ability to be true to that authenticity is all that matters. If I am happy with myself, those around me will benefit from that as well.

You're welcome, world.

Similar to me, there are many parents pleased with their identity. They also insist parenthood is the ultimate job. I will never argue against that.

In my early twenties, I was sitting with a group of people I met through my husband's family friends. I barely knew the family, let alone the friends of the family.

We met at a restaurant in New York City to introduce ourselves before more people joined for the evening. Six women, who were all in their twenties and most of them married, were sitting around a table eating edamame, being friendly and genuine, and having basic conversations about adulting and pressures in life.

One woman was studying for the bar, another had a stressful accounting job, and another woman was becoming a doctor. It was gratifying hearing women discuss struggles and pressures with life. It made me feel less alone and more appreciative of what I've accomplished—although that positivity easily shifted in context that day.

"I have rounds tomorrow morning," the future doctor stated.

"I am burnt out," the future lawyer chimed in.

"We have to keep up this lifestyle for success. My path is planned. Career, marriage, then children," the accountant said.

That same accountant looked at me and said, "What about you, Danielle, what do you do?"

Knowing my career was not as common as theirs, I tried to explain what I did for a living.

"I am an applications technician. I produce household and personal care items and make sure they are stable for consumer use," I proudly said.

"A semi-chemist who makes candles all day?" she questioned with enthusiasm.

I sat there wondering what the heck a semi-chemist was.

"That sounds interesting and fun," the lawyer said.

"Exciting. Not like my stressful life. I would love to have a job like that," the doctor responded.

I sat there trying to digest all the emotional tug of war I was experiencing. Their remarks seemed to downplay my job, yet they generally thought the career path was lively. I didn't know how to react. Defensively, I wanted to prove I did more than make candles for a living, but before I could say anything, I was asked the dreaded question.

"What about children? Do you and Jim want kids?"

At this point I felt drained and slightly degraded.

I quietly shook my head and said, "No."

Cue the awkward tension.

"At least you know what you can handle in life. I wish I didn't have the pressure to prove to my parents I can be their version of responsible," she said.

These backhanded comments were toying with my mind. Was she calling me less responsible compared to her because of my career? Did she think I couldn't handle raising a child? What was this woman's name again? All these questions were like gasoline being poured on a burning fire.

Again, I decided to walk away. No one that insignificant should have the power to impact how you think about yourself, nor do they deserve your attention. The problem is most people judge lifestyles, and deciding to not have a child is not excused from this judgement—it actually amplifies it. There will be many exhausting moments when you are the bigger person, and because of that, you represent character, strength, and resilience.

I do recognize that it can be too much. When those moments occur, don't emotionally argue. Instead, provide calculated debate. Throw that Italian guilt at them, even if you're not Italian. My weapons of choice are real-life examples that contradict judgement.

You don't think I understand what pressure is? OK, let me provide you some insight.

During my dad's illness, I took on the responsibility to support my mom. Though I knew my mom was strong, I also knew she couldn't do this alone. The other half of her life was missing, and she needed support.

Was I fearful my dad was dying? Yes.

Did I worry what life would be like without him? Absolutely.

Had there been a day when I wasn't scared? No.

I needed to accept and address those feelings, being fully aware my mom needed me. I brought her to and from the hospital every day while balancing my full-time job. I made sure my mom took care of herself. I slept at the hospital and at my mom's house from the moment my dad was sick until a few days after his funeral. I discussed all logistics with the doctors, made arrangements for the funeral, grieved, and conducted all the necessary tasks my dad had instructed me to do prior to his hospital admittance. Throughout handling all those responsibilities, the most pressure I had was remembering to care for myself.

Three years later I had the pressure of supporting my husband who almost died of congestive heart failure at the age of forty. During these devastating and emotional times, I was in full support mode, supporting those around me and myself. To feel complete, I had to do whatever it took for my mom to feel less pressure and pain. That provided me the necessary solace during a time of pure sadness.

With Jim's condition, support mode was activated yet again. I was scared, but I oddly approached the situation without fear. I had to. Jim was afraid, our families were thousands of miles away, and the future of his health was unknown. I focused on what was needed for Jim during his recovery after surgeries and embraced the necessary lifestyle changes. Friends supported us by mowing our lawn, bringing food, cleaning the house, and visiting. Family was in constant contact and also made sure I was taking care of myself, which I was. I understood the importance of getting rest, nutrition, and emotional stress relief. I wouldn't be any support to Jim if I ignored myself.

Responsibility is not only about tasks or status but also about accountability and independence. More importantly, it's about the integrity you exemplify while living a trustworthy, dependable life. It's easier to lump responsibilities into hierarchies based on what society has advocated, but life is more granular, and though I don't have the responsibility of raising a child, I am conscientious of the vulnerability, strength, and leadership I've shown thus far in life.

In the end, there are many interpretations of what selfishness is. Selfishness is when I hear parents say a baby can fix their marriage. When does that statement ever end up as a success? In general, research shows children of divorced parents have more behavioral, emotional, and social problems. Even worse, they show emotional disconnect and weaker ties to the parents, especially fathers.[5]

A more definitive example of selfishness is when parents expect their children to take care of them when they grow old.

A few coworkers of mine have honestly stated that having children is a definitive way to ensure you are taken care of. One opinionated, close-minded, coworker was adamant her child's responsibility would be to take care of her as she got older. In fact, that was one reason she decided to have children.

While in the lab, a few people were having miscellaneous conversations while working. A discussion involving a colleague's father who was being cared for by his daughter after he had a stroke prompted a lengthy exchange around children's responsibility regarding their parents. The coworker's father comes from a loving and tight family. There was no debate over why or if the sister supported the father, because the family dynamic presented itself that way. However, the real dispute began when the opinionated, close-minded, coworker stated it was the daughter's obligation to take care of the father. The parents took care of her when she was young, so now it was her duty to pay it forward. According to her, people have children to assure security in the future.

Knowing I didn't have children, she asked me, "Who's going to take care of you when you get older?"

At this point, her comments were directed only at me. Everyone else in the lab was working, while awkwardly ignoring the conversation.

"I don't know. I haven't thought that far ahead," I said.

---

5   Paul Amato, "The Consequences of Divorce and Children," Pennsylvania State University, 2012, https://hrcak.srce.hr/file/180281.

"You will be alone. At least I know my future is set," she confidently said.

Her child was a toddler at the time.

Genuinely annoyed at her thought process, I responded condescendingly, "I didn't know people have children just so they are taken care of when they get older. I didn't think that was a valid reason for having children."

"Wouldn't you want that security?" she quickly quipped.

"How do you know your child will take care of you?" I questioned.

"They should. It is their responsibility," she answered.

Still believing her view was incredibly selfish, I asked, "Don't you think that seems a little selfish and unfair?"

"No. What is wrong with my plan for future security?" she asked angrily.

"Your child might have a problem with it," I said.

She scoffed, "He won't. I will be living with my son, and you will be in some nursing home alone."

"Well, at least I will be with good company," I retaliated.

What I struggle to understand are the popular rules for defining selfishness. Why am I selfish for not having a child, while a mother who has a child so she is taken care of is not? Why is it selfish to say I love myself more than my desire to have a child? Why is my decision to not have a child considered selfish, yet people worry I will be alone? Why is my calculated, rationalized decision, which was made while weighing the consequences, emotions, and loved ones' opinions, viewed as being self-absorbed?

I chose to not be a mom, an opportunity that a large part of society deems important to life, and sometimes that sacrifice is viewed as self-centered. I can assure you that my decision was not due to self-indulgence. Those who know their importance think of others, while those who think they are important only think of themselves.

Despite what many people think, it isn't selfish for *you* to live as you wish; it's selfish asking *others* to live as you wish.

Chapter 6
FAMILY

"Who will continue the family traditions and namesake?"

To me, family is extremely important, and though many people did not experience a childhood straight out of a '90s family sitcom, I was lucky enough to live episodes from the lives of the Seavers, Keatons, and Tanners.

Anytime my sisters or I were in a situation, our parents would be there supporting us, teaching us a lesson and having us learn from our mistakes. My parents' opened their home to our friends multiple times when they needed a place to stay. Some stayed for weeks, others a year. No questions were asked—just a request to respect my parents' rules and values while our friends worked on their situation. Why? Because my parents' character was enriched with pure virtue, empathy, and encouragement.

Basically, everywhere you look, everywhere you go, there's a heart and a hand to hold onto. As long as we keep on giving, we can take anything that comes our way, rain or shine. We got each other sharing laughter and love.

For those not familiar with that sappy explanation, research the theme songs for the television shows *Full House* and *Growing Pains*.

Once you hear those lyrics, I guarantee your mind will have them on repeat for the rest of the day.

This upbringing makes it easy to answer those who question whether my childhood played a role in my decision to not have children.

Absolutely not.

My childhood was amazing. I was loved, taught values, held responsibilities, created awesome memories, and was surrounded by people I still speak with to this day. With morals instilled, I witnessed what family and determination delivers in life.

My mom and dad, who are the epitome of love, met in high school and were together until my dad's death fifty years later. They raised their children with family being the core value. I grew up in a typical half-German, half-Italian, household, which meant a *very* close family and never a dull moment—always loud, always eating, using any excuse to simply get together.

Family Sundays were at Noni's, and every week when I walked into that house, I smelled the sauce (not gravy) and heard everyone downstairs in the second kitchen.

For those who are not Italian, let me take a page from Sophia Petrillo's book from the television show *The Golden Girls*. Picture it: an Italian household where there's an upstairs (and downstairs) kitchen, a minimum of three refrigerators, twenty uncles and cousins named Joe, and the push to *mangiare* (eat). Uncle Joe is sitting at the head of the table with his *Milwaukee's Best*, eating peanuts, while Pop Pop completes his word search wearing his green visor at the other end of the table. All my remarkably close cousins are running around in chaos at the heart of the family!

My dad's side also has a family bond with amazing traditions and love—not to mention tempers! Now, don't get me wrong: the Milazzo side had tempers, but the Schwartz side patented the trait. Unfortunately, I never knew my dad's parents. They passed away shortly after I was born, only a few months apart. My poor dad and his sister, Dorothy, endured such loss and pain in a short amount of time. The family supported one another, and the bonds provided significant support. Oddly enough, that family bond was challenged again when both my dad and my aunt passed away within the same year.

My father's family was older and more spread out across the country, yet some of my greatest memories revolved around my Aunt Dorothy, her husband Bobby, and their children Donna, Robby, and Kim.

Pulling up to her house every Fourth of July in Montclair, New Jersey, you would find a crowd of people outside on the porch. Family, neighbors, and friends all hung out next to the lineup of coolers and tables filled with homemade delicious food. The back door with the diamond window was constantly ajar to allow the bombardment of incredible food made lovingly by family.

After the wonderment in the kitchen was done, Dorothy—who loved red lipstick, dressed to impress, and baked the best chocolate mousse—embraced the environment she created. We all watched the parade make its way down the street and continued to gather until the night mosquitos pushed us out.

During our drive home, though sad to leave, I was always excited to see the Macy's Fourth of July fireworks in the distance. Without fail, every year, I remember thinking how grateful I was for my family and that porch.

I am the youngest of three daughters. Some might say I am the favorite. Others, to this day, call me "the baby." I looked at it as keeping my parents young. Dorene and I are separated in age by ten years, while Dawn and I are fourteen years apart.

Can someone say oopsie-baby?

My sisters and my mom look identical, and then there is me—always being questioned if I am related. It isn't until someone sees a picture of my dad and they see the resemblance that I'm allowed to put those milkman rumors to rest!

In the past I've looked toward Dawn as a mother figure, while Dorene and I had the sibling relationship.

When I was twelve, Dawn took me to Disney World for the first time, without our parents. She had the overall responsibility to watch over me. Mom and Dad trusted her with such precious cargo! Dawn always considered me with her plans. Wherever and whatever she and her now husband did, they made sure I was a part of the situation. She was compassionate, protective, defensive, and proud of me. At any moment Dawn would boastfully speak to her friends about me and truly show happiness and love for me having been born.

Meanwhile, my relationship with Dorene revolves around memories of sibling fighting, jealousy, and protection. If you don't have a sibling, imagine a person who at any given time you can freely talk to, laugh at, fight with, cry on, hate toward, love, and protect. The mood of the day dictates the relationship, with the bond being undeniably strong.

I remember one instance where Dorene was marinating a roast. I can't recall why I was so mad, but the fight was intense, causing me to throw the roast on the floor. I was seven, and she was seventeen. She probably was teasing me or bossing me around, and I retaliated by disrespecting her hard work. I was in the wrong, but I can guarantee you she antagonized me to the point of action. Why? Because we are sisters. Yet for all the delicious, marinated carcasses tossed on the floor, there were moments of protection that followed.

When I was ten years old, my sister Dorene was dating a firefighter. I hung out with them a few times, and my gut told me my sister was going to get hurt. To me he didn't seem trustworthy, but to her he was perfect.

One day, sitting on the wall outside our house, I told my sister's boyfriend he wasn't good enough for her. I figured if no one else was going to say it, I would. Since I was a kid, he brushed my thoughts aside and ignored me. To assure him I wasn't joking, I poured lemonade on his walkie talkie. Now that I think about it, why was my go-to move destroying other people's belongings? It doesn't matter. That tactic was effective. He was so pissed that his reaction opened my sister's eyes.

My instinct was correct; he wasn't good enough for her. Moments like those prove it doesn't matter if I was ten or one hundred and ten: I will always protect my sisters and family.

This is a fair warning for everyone to hide your meats and refreshing beverages.

Memories are important factors in my life, and thanks to my dad, I will always have documented ones. My dad went everywhere with a video camera. My family, friends, even my neighbors all knew that the moment a tripod and gigantic light came out, the camera was turning on. It also meant that there would be some cursing and anxiety, since technology in the eighties and nineties never worked smoothly. To this day, if I see someone recording on a video camera, I experience a slew of emotions. Usually, I smile with happiness because I automatically think of my dad—a father who would do anything for his children. He had so much kindness, love, and family dedication. When I say I had the best dad, I truly did. But that damn video camera also brought anxiety and stress. My pops wanted to capture every situation, and if something went wrong, denying him that moment, the Schwartz temper came out. Just to clarify, there was no violence, just a lot of angry yelling, passion, and swearing. This caused an atmosphere once surrounded with joy to pivot into an environment of awkwardness and apprehension. Because that camera was everywhere in our lives, that restlessness happened a lot, which boiled over to this day.

When I feel stress, those feelings shift to pure sadness, heartache, and grief, knowing my dad—the best dad ever—is gone. Though my father and some family members are no longer physically with us, those videos provide wonderful moments that connect me. I saw my Nana and Pop for the first time through one of those powerful lenses. They held me as a baby, and I heard my grandmother's infectious and boisterous laugh (something I now know I inherited).

One thing is certain: a camera was not needed to remember my childhood—playing with Matchbox cars (don't even think about giving me a Barbie), hanging outside with the same group of friends, watching Saturday morning cartoons, taking care of my Cabbage Patch Kids, doing small chores, walking to school, and playing sports. Let me take a moment to mention *Captain Caveman*, *Smurfs*, *Duck Tales*, *Snorks*, *Fragile Rock*, *Jem*, *ThunderCats*, *GI Joe*, *Transformers*, and the TGIF lineup; these were some of the best television shows and held a huge influence on my childhood!

Not only did I grow up with amazing cartoons, I also had great childhood friends. All coming from different cultures, backgrounds, and beliefs, we held the overall same respect for one another. Although we all have grown, that sense of pure emotion and respect is sincere. When there is happiness in our lives, we smile. When there is grief, we're sad. When there is hate, we're angered. It isn't because we are still best friends; it's simply because in our small diverse town, we had the privilege of surrounding each other with common humanity, morals, and integrity.

My parents worked ridiculously hard to provide for their family, and it wasn't about materialistic items. It was about my dad driving us to the public beach where he would sit all day in the hot sand that he hated, in his long Docker pants and shoes, just to see us smile. Or better yet, making it a point at 6 p.m. to provide a homecooked dinner around the table.

I have been lucky to experience my family and childhood upbringing, although knowing that my decision to not have children prevents those traditions from being passed down creates sadness within. Of course, I want every child to encounter such amazingness that correlates to adulthood, but even that desire is faint compared to *my* version of a fulfilled life.

I met a woman in an airport while waiting for our delayed flight, and we struck up a conversation about family. She was on her way to visit her daughter and son-in-law, and I was returning home from seeing my family. Both of us showed pride and shared a glimpse into our households with smiles that beamed from the gate to the runway. For half an hour, it was a family-consumed conversation. Oddly enough, I was never asked if I had children but felt attached to hers. It was a sense of community, familiarity, and connection. This engagement is similar to a sense of belonging. The sense that you are a part of something or someone that thoroughly accepts traditions and provides fulfillment.

Belonging is a fundamental part of being human, and when people lack that sense, it is a strong predictor of depression. Being identified with a group setting even outside of a family—church, work, clubs, group chats, or even hobbyists—provides a necessary importance for our behavior, resiliency, and both our physical and mental health.[1]

Am I sad that the Tsao and, especially, Schwartz last names will not be carried on by Jim and me? Yes. However, that sense of sadness lessens knowing my sisters and family are raising their children with the same values and traditions I experienced.

Making this complicated decision and knowing Jim and I will not experience significant moments is challenging. To help ease that difficulty, I triumph through acceptance, which empowers my growth. By truly accepting my authentic self, I actively identify ways to improve reality. The makeup of life is your experiences, setbacks, family, community, and abilities wherein specific circumstances, acceptance allows decisions. In my existence, I accept myself for everything I am and everything I am not, including being a mother.

Author and entrepreneur Rachel Cargle runs the Instagram account Rich Auntie Supreme,[2] a forum dedicated to highlighting the image of blissful, carefree women who can live that way due to their child-free lifestyle. Rachel, being child-free, discusses the variety of ways to caretake and be present in kids' lives. She chose to live child-free and accepted this as an invitation to have relationships with kids without

---

1 Tracy Brower, "Missing Your People: Why Belonging Is So Important and How To Create It," *Forbes*, January 10, 2021, http://www.forbes.com/sites/tracybrower/2021/01/10/missing-your-people-why-belonging-is-so-important-and-how-to-create-it/?sh=1a544fb47c43.

2 Rachel Cargle (@richauntiesupreme), https://www.instagram.com/richauntiesupreme/.

being a parent. "Having children in your world is a meaningful part of the life experience."[3] She goes on to explain how one can embrace this wonderment through the "auntie" or "uncle" route, but this role comes with responsibilities, and to ensure consistent involvement, there are five necessary steps one "auntie" or "uncle" should consider.

1. Figure out your role: The great part about not being a parent is that you can choose your level of engagement. How involved do you want to be, and what does that look like?

2. Come up with a routine for staying in touch: Once you figure out your role, think about how often you want to live that.

3. Provide non-judgmental support: You can provide different outlooks and considerations without being held responsible or accountable. You're not the parent or primary caretaker. Instead, you are in the safe zone.

4. Have a conversation about boundaries with the child and their parents: Sure, you can be the safe, fun aunt, but be open and communicate with the child's parents if you feel morals, values, or safety are being challenged or jeopardized.

5. Talk about discipline: Discuss with the parents what type of discipline they are OK with. Because you are in a safe zone, children might push the boundaries. Having an understanding of acceptable limits and punishment is necessary.

I love being a fun auntie—not only to my nephews, but to my friends' and other family members' children as well. Having that ability to be a part of their lives while handing them back to their respective parents is extremely fulfilling to me. For those who allow me to take on an aunt role in their child's life, I'm also willing to handle the not-so-fun responsibilities too: Changing diapers, holding screaming babies, and cleaning up vomit all come with the territory, and I am here for that!

---

3   Mayowa Aina, "How to be an amazing auntie or uncle," *NPR*, August 13, 2023.

I was hanging out with my young nephew, Max, and my sister Dorene. Max was eating chicken nuggets when all of a sudden, he started to choke. Without hesitation, I opened his mouth, looked in his airway, and used my finger to scoop out the chicken nugget and confirm he was breathing.

Now to some this might seem like common sense, but Max was the first small child I'd had experience with. To not panic and to know exactly what to do to keep him calm was significant. Not to mention that saliva, chewed-up food, and germs gross me out. But all that didn't matter. Instincts kicked in, and protection came out.

My other nephew, Ryan, always listened when I babysat him. He trusted me with everything, and he was not problematic. He was constantly on his best behavior, and I believe he enjoyed our time together and never wanted to disappoint me, though I can't say his parents experience the same thing. We are great buds, which is another wonderful benefit of being a fun, cool aunt.

I am more patient with kids than adults, and they seem to be comfortable around me. Funnily enough for not wanting children, my husband and I are godparents to many. God forbid something were to happen, Jim and I would be looking at a basketball team lineup. I guess it's fitting, since Jim and I like sports.

What's also fitting is marrying my best friend over a decade ago, and it has been a continuous adventure ever since. We have similar interests: sports, travel, and food, along with our own guilty pleasures—his being video games and mine being reality television. Jim and I balance each other out, but it isn't necessarily easy. It is a constant upward journey we travel during the stages in our life. But honestly, even after twenty-plus years, I still get excited when he gets home. Because without him, our home is just a house.

For those worried a child-free marriage will not be plentiful, without a doubt Jim is enough for my life. He fulfills my happiness through his love, conversations, and presence. His constant support during my career moves and entrepreneur adventures instills confidence in me.

His acceptance and encouragement for me to be the loud and abrasive figure in the relationship shows he understands and embraces who I am. Jim challenges me by calling out my faults, especially when I overexaggerate or am too sympathetic, blinded by bias, or too afraid. He admires my tenaciousness, my ability to handle pressure, and how I challenge myself. He defends me in any instance necessary and suffers when I am suffering. Most importantly, he makes it known through words, hugs, or surprises how lucky and proud he is of his best friend.

Jim has been on my adulting roller coaster since I was nineteen. He knows me better than anyone else. To put things into perspective, my life started off similar to a mini roller coaster you might find on a boardwalk. These rides typically don't have steep hills or loops but sudden, aggressive turns that give you whiplash and shake you with uncertainty.

When we first started dating, I found myself living the college life; then I graduated and was thrown into adulthood with no straight or stable paths.

The next amusement around my mid-twenties resembled a wooden roller coaster—usually fast with entertaining hills but not cushioned well enough to avoid bruises from the short-lived thrill. This fast-paced part of my life had many career rejections and soul searches, all while staying afloat with bills.

My late twenties would be the Great American Scream Machine at Great Adventure in New Jersey. Built with mainstream loops, maximum height, and excessive speed, it was an invigorating and exploratory ride. However, the excessive force of this roller coaster pushed you to your limit, demanding plans to revolve around this beast. Without a doubt, this resembled my ticket to Cadbury, where I was provided a career, exclusive knowledge, a working family, global exposures, and significant challenges.

The current roller coaster of life is similar to Steel Force at Cedar Point in Ohio, a steep, classic thrill ride filled with adrenaline and no significant surprises. Just memorable moments of feeling like you are on top of the world. Established, confident, comfortable, and explorative: this is me now, both professionally and personally.

Through my tracks of life, no matter how chaotic and nerve-wracking, invigorating and new, or classic and impressive, Jim has had a seat right next to me. That support is used to answer those who question if my marriage is strong enough for a child. Yes, Jim and I are strong— assemble-IKEA-furniture-together-and-not-get-divorced strong!

Jim and I nailed it (literally)!

What I do find interesting are the people who assume a marriage with problems can be solved by having a child.

A friend and her partner were going through some difficult times. They accidentally got pregnant and had a baby. According to her, that miracle changed their relationship for the better. The focus and bond were strictly on the child but not their problems. It was a temporary fix without solving core issues. I wish I could say that this was just my opinion, but the couple divorced when the child was two.

Research on marriage and children has found negative relations between variables. Parenthood was associated with decreased marriage quality, increased marital conflict, more severe symptoms of depression, and decreased marital satisfaction, especially when pregnancy was unplanned.[4]

Not only is raising children time-consuming and tiring, it is also related to frequent exposure of stressors. In most instances, adding a child is not the solution for marital problems. Even if partners are fulfilled as parents, their relational well-being may be threatened due to parental distress. Of course each situation is subjective and unique; however, parents can experience greater stress from finances, more worry based on the child's safety, increased struggles to meet demands of modern-day parenting, greater fatigue, and sadness due to feelings

4   Marta Kowal et al., "When and how does the number of children affect marital satisfaction? An international survey," *PLOS ONE*, April 22, 2021, https://doi.org/10.1371/journal.pone.0249516.

of disappointment stemming from their performance as parents and balancing life.[5]

This stress is felt behind closed doors and is sometimes on full display in public. I have seen many couples disagree over parenting, fighting over money, religion, dominance, and parenting technique— coddling versus experiencing life, loose versus strict rules, or enforcer versus friend and the good cop/bad cop relationship. With the addition of a child, it isn't uncommon for the couple to forget they were partners before they were parents.

Then there are times when being a partner is not enough. There are those who state marriage is for the sanctity of procreation, and in their eyes, that is the truth. In general, we all need to remember not everyone has the same viewpoint or beliefs, although admittedly, it may be hard for people to have an open mind, especially when influential figures loudly disagree with such a personal viewpoint.

In early 2022, Pope Francis criticized couples who choose to have pets instead of children as selfish, arguing that their decision to forgo parenthood leads to a loss of humanity and is a detriment to civilization.

OUCH.

Not to mention this statement is coming from someone who most consider a progressive pontiff.

"Today we see a form of selfishness. We see that people do not want to have children, or just one and no more. And many, many, couples do not have children because they do not want to, or they have just one—but they have two dogs, two cats . . . Yes, dogs and cats take the place of children. . . . And this denial of fatherhood or motherhood diminishes us; it takes away our humanity. And in this way civilization becomes aged and without humanity, because it loses the richness of

5   Daniela Veronica Negraia and Jennifer March Augustine, "Unpacking the Parenting Well-Being Gap: the Role of Dynamic Features of Daily Life Across Broader Social Contexts," *Social Psychology Quarterly* (June 10, 2020), https://journals.sagepub.com/doi/10.1177/0190272520902453.

fatherhood and motherhood. And our homeland suffers, as it does not have children."[6]

How am I, or anyone else who lives a carefully determined child-free life, advocating for ourselves when prominent figures are loudly declaring antagonistic subjective viewpoints—beliefs that clearly have a lapse in understanding a person whose value, moral standing, and character is not defined by parenthood. It is a constant battle that requires childless people to have their defense argument ready at any given moment, patience when communicating and explaining their decision, and most importantly, the courage to demonstrate their authenticity and self-confidence.

Obviously my three adorable fur babies are not tiny humans; however, they are a part of my family and heart. They emotionally communicate a wide range of feelings through specific meow pitches and show love with warm purrs and gentle nudges. I constantly change the litter and feed, play, worry, protect, and love those four-legged beautiful souls. Financially they cost thousands of dollars for medical surgeries and treatments, such as premature periodontal disease, kitty allergies, and polydactyly toe removal, just to name a few. They're territorial, picky eaters, demonstrate favoritism, and exhibit separation anxiety when I try to go to the bathroom alone. They're also comforting, intuitive, and protective, and they force me to take them into consideration regarding the future. Watching them grow up is an illustrious experience, and when that unavoidable time comes that they cross over the rainbow bridge, a part of my life will become empty. No, I am not a mother, per say, but these fur monsters are my children and a part of humanity. You can mock it, challenge it, or follow the pope's idealization by blaming it. Nevertheless, that shade will not change how intricate those kitties are in my life, nor will it allow you to escape my momma bear defense.

---

6   Joshua Berlinger, "Opting for pets over children is selfish and 'takes away our humanity,' says Pope Francis," *CNN*, January 5, 2022, http://edition.cnn.com/2022/01/05/europe/pope-dogs-cats-kids-intl/index.html.

Some religions have also demonstrated that sex should be for procreation only and contraception is the "devil's candy."

Previously I explained how alcohol is framed by some as the "devil's juice," and now this— an absolute true experience I had witnessing an anti-Planned Parenthood rally in Arkansas.

I was stuck in traffic while driving to dinner one night after a manufacturing trial. I rolled down my window and could hear the protestors next to my car screaming their chant with their fists flaring and wide eyes glaring: "CONTRACEPTION IS THE DEVIL'S CANDY!"

It was a little terrifying, but at the same time, I found it hilarious. No matter whether I agree or not, I should show respect and not laugh at the image I pictured inside my head: The devil handing women all types of weird, flavored contraceptives, similar to the jelly beans that taste like dishwater or stink bug.

No matter the flavor of life, I am going to respect it as your view. Some passionately believe contraceptives prevent God's plan, while others politely disagree and use that "evil" confection as protection.

A few women and families that I've met through work travels and friend acquaintances, both in the US and globally, were adamant a child must be part of the marriage equation. A woman whose sister married into a family with extremely strict beliefs stated her sister needed to be a virgin before she could get married, and prior to marriage her fertility health must be examined and confirmed by a doctor. IVF or any other medical fertility treatments were against their religious beliefs.

"If my sister cannot conceive naturally, her future husband is allowed to find someone who can provide that option," she said calmly.

"Would she stay together with the husband?" I asked.

"They can remain married but with an open relationship. My sister cannot accuse her husband of infidelity," she explained.

"Would the other woman be a part of the family and raise the baby?" I asked.

"Yes, that woman is part of the family. She would be the mother of the child, but my sister would be the woman of the house," she stated.

Honestly, I couldn't believe I was hearing this type of arrangement in the United States. As ignorant as my statement sounds, I only knew beliefs like this existed in other parts of the world, not so close to home.

Other times, situations are experienced all too often. The constant pressure from family and society enables decisions which force some to contemplate the what-ifs.

A cashier at a grocery store I frequently visited was outside on her break. Through small talk, the topic of children came up. The only thing I knew about this woman was that she grew up in a small town, had children, and wore a gold cross around her neck.

"Do you have children?" she asked while smoking a cigarette.

"No, no children for me," I said.

"Do you want children?" she asked while she exhaled cigarette smoke.

"No. My husband and I are happy without children," I answered.

"That's awesome. You know what you both want!" she exclaimed.

"Yes, we decided a long time ago we did not want children, and we never looked back," I said.

"I do have children," she mentioned. "I never wanted any, but I was pressured my whole life to have kids. My family, my husband, my friends all wanted me to have kids," she explained.

"It's hard dealing with that type of pressure," I emphasized.

"I admire you for knowing what you want and who you are. Don't get me wrong; I love my children, but I always wonder what if," she stated.

Her last statement, "I always wonder what if," is a feeling I try to avoid. Life is too short to question matters afterwards and too complicated not to question at all.

Other marriage-related comments focus on Jim and me as an interracial couple. Jim is Asian, and I am Caucasian. Insert first stereotype here: "But your children would be so smart!"

Sure!

There is no doubt in my mind our children would be intelligent. Not to mention tenacious, respectful, and curious. If they couldn't learn something, they wouldn't give up. They would fully embrace and own their uniqueness, all while treating people with humility and regard. Despite knowing my child would be astute, it is not a formidable reason to have a kid.

Insert stereotype number two: "Aren't you curious about what your biracial child would look like?"

Absolutely!

My whole life people have stated interracial kids hit the genetic appearance jackpot. If Jim and I had children, I can't disagree with that statement. Jim is handsome and looks young, while I have a nice smile and a uniquely dimpled chin. However, that curiosity holds zero significance regarding my decision.

Jim and I take full advantage of our choice to not have children. We have flexibility and reduce the stress in our lives by communicating what is important to us both individually and as a unit. One shouldn't forget that marriage is complicated without children. It takes hard work to maintain the union, and finding that right balance of individuality and togetherness can take a lifetime together.

So far, my wedding was the best day of my life. Not just because it was a blast (because it was) or had incredible food (because it did), but because it was the first day of my marriage.

The venue we picked was beautiful both inside and out. The outside area where we were to get married was dripping with beautiful flowers and a well-manicured landscape.

Purely picturesque.

The inside was just as beautiful: grand ceilings, chandeliers designed for royalty, and large rooms to accommodate any size crowd. Good thing, since the two hundred guests weren't able to enjoy the outside at all. Mother Nature, on that particular June day, decided to provide our wedding present in the form of forty-degree weather, torrential rain, and sixty mile-per-hour winds—all day. You know how they say that rain on your wedding day is good luck? Well, Jim and I were blessed with an exorbitant amount. It didn't matter. After ten years of dating, we were excited to officially become husband and wife in front of all our friends and family. Jim didn't see my dress or me before our ceremony. His expression of pure happiness matched mine the moment those doors opened and my dad walked me down the aisle. Our vows, though short and sweet, were simply us. Nothing romantic, just realistic. We don't need one another—we *choose* to be with each other. We incorporated some of his Asian culture into our reception, such as bamboo centerpieces, tea party favors, and red and gold colors. I ate until my dress felt too tight, but I was still able to dance the night away. Our official reception ended at midnight; however, many of us celebrated our unity with an after party at a dance lounge where their closing song at 3 a.m. was "I'm Yours," by Jason Mraz. Thirty great friends in a circle on the dance floor, all holding hands, swaying and singing the lyrics to Jim and me, who were in the center of this epic moment. One of the many amazing memories from that evening.

While Jim and I continue to create amazing memories and navigate, we know not to half-ass two things but to whole-ass one thing. For us, the whole ass is our marriage, and that is enough.

Chapter 7
CIRCLE OF LIFE

"Are you afraid of growing old alone?"

Growing up, you're introduced to stories, cartoons, and relatable characters. On top of that, you find yourself jamming away to common melodies that captivate for a lifetime. From Humpty Dumpty sitting on a wall, to that twinkle of the little star, everyone recognizes the tune or knows the lyrics. Case in point, take a moment and sing the nursery rhyme designed to outline life's ideal plan:

> *Danielle and Jim,*
> *Sitting in a tree,*
> *K-I-S-S-I-N-G,*
> *First comes love,*
> *Then comes marriage,*
> *Then comes the baby in the baby carriage!*

Well, this just got awkward.

Even though this catchy jingle is sometimes used to embarrass people, from an early age it has been engraved in our minds, similar to the Pledge of Allegiance. I haven't recited the Pledge of Allegiance in a while, yet my first attempt flowed as if no time had passed. Don't get me wrong; not all remembrances compared to our patriotic statement are important, yet their influential significance can heavily weigh on societal direction.

A young Danielle in pigtails remembers listening, memorizing, and even singing along to life's ideal nursery rhyme. As I got older, I realized preconceived notions thrusted upon us can diminish in validity over time.

Something that doesn't diminish is the challenge in life to be yourself, especially in a world that is trying to make you like everyone else. I believe you should care and focus on that statement versus making sure you fit a dated standard, social norm, or overall pressure. Group pressure is enormously effective in producing social conformity and powerful enough to alter humans' perception of reality.[1] While each of us holds responsibility for our own choices, understanding the role social pressure plays is profoundly imperative. It can unwillingly force resistance to grow, increase the necessity to fit in, and decrease independent decisions. I know it's difficult coloring outside the lines and going against social norms, but imagine a world if Picasso didn't?

When people ask how I face challenging the social expectations of motherhood, I typically relate my response to something familiar to them: their child's aspirations.

When parenting, do they tell their hopeful kiddos their fate is based on what society dictates, or do they encourage them to have ambitions, a voice, and individual thoughts?

Of course, no parent wants to dampen their child's eagerness. Instead, they press for individualism. The same stands for me. I want to conform based on what's best for me, not what society deems as correct.

I am blessed in a way that I don't feel obligated to blend in with all societal pressures, though it wasn't an easy journey. I am consciously defying a common definition and global acceptance by loudly portraying my authenticity, beliefs, and own acceptance.

---

1   Better Help Editorial Team, "Impacts Of Social Pressure," *Better Help*, April 4, 2024, https://www.betterhelp.com/advice/general/how-does-social-pressure-impact-our-choices/.

Acceptance is key, even with complicated topics such as the environment. Some people are choosing not to have children because they fear doing so will amplify global warming. From CO_2 emissions to extreme weather events that may force future children to endure a negative lifestyle, more people are determining these environmental impacts to be detrimental.

In a 2019 Instagram live stream to her 1.5 million followers, thirty-four-year-old US representative Alexandria Ocasio-Cortez said: "Basically, there's a scientific consensus that the lives of children are going to be exceedingly difficult. And it does lead, I think, young people to have a legitimate question: "Is it OK to still have children?"[2]

I ran into a woman on the West Coast who decided she did not want to have children because of the overall population and environment.

With a passionate tone she asked, "Are you afraid the earth is overpopulated?"

Knowing the world *is* overpopulated but believing in the circle of life, I responded, "Yes, but I believe the complex system will balance out."

Possibly my response sounded naïve to her, as she quickly defended her choice to not have children.

"The world is grossly overpopulated. Not to mention the significant suffering and unavoidable environmental decline," she passionately stated.

We chatted more about her life, and I felt comfortable asking if she would consider adoption.

"Children are not a must-have in my life, but adoption would be a consideration after I accomplish my bucket list," she confidently expressed.

For those dying in anticipation, some items on this woman's bucket list included Pacific Coast beach cleanup and Habitat for Humanity.

---

2   Sam Shead, "Climate change is making people think twice about having children," CNBC, August 21, 2021, https://www.cnbc.com/2021/08/12/climate-change-is-making-people-think-twice-about-having-children.html.

As I heard her selfless bucket list, I hoped she didn't ask about mine. Then it happened.

"What is on your bucket list?" she inquired.

Dreading the comparison between my bucket list and hers, I took a deep sigh with my head down and quietly stated, "Skydiving and global travel."

Why was it so easy to automatically judge myself in a negative light? At that moment, I turned into everyone who has judged me to be materialistic. It is important to recognize how frequently these situations will occur, even if you are the most secure and defined person. Take a breath and remember to measure all that defines you. Sure, the bucket list from the surface seems luxurious, simply because I understand the correlation of fun elements to a fulfilled life. For me, enjoyable activities are just as important as delivering key responsibilities. This balance supports my lifestyle and the continuous momentum of overall acceptance.

With my child-free life choices, more times than not, people state that I am depriving the world of future possibilities. Apparently, my unborn child has the potential to discover the cure for cancer. Maybe, or maybe my kid would be a lazy piece of crap! (Who am I kidding? My kid would be awesome!)

So here is my apology to the universe:

Dear World,

I am sorry that you are missing out on an extraordinary human being, but frankly I think he or she would be too much for you to handle. So, in retrospect, you're welcome.

Sincerely,

Danielle

One thing I don't want to miss out on are equal circumstances. Just because I decided to not have a child does not mean I am available to stay late at work or come in early during a snowstorm. My decision to not have a child is not the company's solution to support substandard long-term situations. Why are child-related excuses more valid and lenient than mine? Don't get me wrong; I understand that some instances require parents to leave work at random times, and with my work ethic, I will push to get the job done effectively and efficiently. However, why does the entire office need to stay late to hit a deadline unless you have a child? What if you have a sick pet, a scheduled obligation, or even an anniversary? In my past experiences, after I pleaded my case, I usually had a fifty-fifty chance of getting approval to leave— zero out of a hundred if a parent had already left. Luckily for child-free workers, time is allowing for positive changes in work-life balance, but there are still significant areas for improvement.

Time is not a guarantee but a borrowed gift, and I feel a lot of people assume tomorrow is a given. Instead, one should remember the past, live in the present, and hope for the future. If I am lucky enough to grow old, I envision it with Jim. Despite the positive thoughts, I can't escape the inevitable. My family is becoming smaller each year, and with no children to possibly support me in the future, I could grow old alone.

At least from a societal point of view, there has been more encouragement and support for older adults to stay active in the workplace, increased policies to better protect senior citizens, and positive movements in states focusing on friendlier city attributes such as transportation, restaurants, and shopping centers. Also, to target a more enriched life for the elderly, there has been positive growth around improved education and training, diverse staff hiring, increased salary, and better facility amenities within nursing homes and active senior centers. What the aging demographics really call upon is for everyone to think in advance and see population aging as an opportunity for positive change.[3]

As of now, I see it as me being the life of the party at the Shady Pines nursing home!

---

3   Marcia Ory, "How Will Society Change As The U.S. Population Ages?", *Texas A& M Today*, Sept 28, 2020, https://today.tamu.edu/2020/09/28/how-will-society-change-as-the-u-s-population-ages/.

One must understand judgements will happen no matter how old you are.

An older female coworker who never had children was at a lake party celebrating Memorial Day when the conversation of family was brought up.

"Tracy, do you have children?" a woman asked.

"No, I never had children," she happily replied.

A woman who has been known to hate Tracy swooped into the conversation to poke the bear.

"Tracy, you are by yourself at your age?" she condescendingly asked.

"I'm not alone; I have my husband and family," Tracy said calmly.

"Well, your husband is older too. Good luck growing old. I feel for you," the other woman sarcastically said.

I'd had enough of this woman's disingenuous attitude.

"OK, that's enough," I said while holding my hand up to the middle of the circle.

Acting as if she didn't know her comments were negative, the woman automatically replied with a passive-aggressive response. "Oh, I am sorry. I wasn't trying to offend. I was merely pointing out the obvious. You see, my son just bought me a house, and when that time comes, he will move in to take care of me. I have that security and love. Tracy doesn't, and I'm just worried for her. That's all."

Tracy was standing there tall and strong. How was she not screaming?

After the woman believed her point was made, she sipped her glass of wine and left the circle. Tracy turned to me, took a sip of her drink, and proceeded to show me how to be the boss of any situation.

"Danielle, don't believe everything you hear, and don't let insignificance control your dominance," Tracy said.

"OK, but how can you do that with such nastiness in your face?" I asked.

Tracy pulled down her sunglasses, stared directly in my eyes, smirked, and stated, "That woman paints a picture of an ideal life. The truth is she paid for that house with her divorce settlement. And her son is moving in because his cheating girlfriend kicked him out after confessing the baby she's carrying is not his."

Tracy put her sunglasses back on, finished her drink, and walked away with an enormous amount of confidence.

Sometimes from alternate views, life's ideal plan seems remarkable, but reality proves it to be unattainable. That is why it is important for individuals to develop and live their own ideal version. It takes adaptability, strength, and confidence to define your path, especially knowing people grow up, friends grow apart, and life travels in multiple directions.

With my direction, it's obvious I don't have children, but that doesn't mean I only relate to those who also don't have children. The people I know who have children take some needed time for themselves. They occasionally trade in the G-rated *Baby Shark* life for an R-rated rom com and communicate in grown-up verbal diarrhea versus the baby talk drool.

Keep in mind that even if my circle of friends discusses children, I can still follow or engage in the conversation. Granted, do I want to consistently hear about all the coos and cahs or view two thousand pictures of the most "beautiful baby in the world"? No, but that doesn't mean I'm not interested. Do I want to get milk drunk over your fatigue or how your body has been completely destroyed? Nope. Whatever the conversation might be, I am committed because I am your friend. I will listen, provide a shoulder to cry on, and be present in moments important to you. I guarantee you the majority of parents will want to discuss something different than organic diaper rash recipes or their frustration with the baked good selection at the school PTA.

When I moved to Wisconsin, I met this group of amazing women. Smart, funny, fierce, and fabulous. Some were starting their families, some trying to decide if they wanted children, and others establishing their boss behavior! We came from different areas of life but somehow seemed to be the missing pieces in our ideal life journey.

Early on at our job, we were associated as a whole, even when some of us left the company. But a comment from a former senior leader has always stuck with me.

"It is good you found friends, but in general it's usually temporary," he said. "The group will move on to other things, especially growing a family, and you'll only be left with memories."

Apparently, he experienced this in his life and learned to only count on himself. Though I can see similarities with our child-free decisions, that was the only common attribute. I allow others into my life with full expectations they will go onto something larger. I wouldn't expect anything less, and I assure you, I will be their biggest supporter.

With this coworker, though, he actively separated himself from anything not his lifestyle. There might be instances in my life where I detach, but those who I genuinely care about will always be a part of my ideal life plan. With this Wisco Disco group, I will never be alone.

Family and friends are significant in my life, but I am whole just being me. This bold feeling and expression can cause arguments. Some fear I can't feel whole unless I experience that unconditional love a child provides. Many women have told me the moment they held their newborn was the very first time they experienced unconditional love—an undeniable, unforgettable bond. As for me, I am not afraid of missing out on this connection since I've never had or wanted it. Plus, I am overflowing with love from my family, friends, fur babies and husband. In the mind of some parents, that experience might not be the same, but for me, it's all I need.

Fear is a loaded word commonly summarized as an automatic emotional reaction to a perceived danger or threat. Fear prepares us to react to danger by slowing or shutting down functions not needed for survival and sharpening attributes for a more efficient reaction. However, chronic exposure to fear can provide physical ailments such as a weakened immune system, cardiovascular damage, memory impairment, and mental health.[4]

I am human, so it is inevitable I have fears, but how can I tell the difference between a fear and a phobia? The difference is simple. Fears are common reactions to events or objects. But a fear becomes a phobia when it interferes with your ability to function and maintain a consistent quality of life.[5]

For me, cruise ships are a phobia. I experience significant anxiety when I see large cruise ships. I have never physically been on one before, but for some reason just the sight of the monstrous floating petri dish causes me to tense up and become overwhelmed with urgency, panic, and sadness, to the point where my friends and I try to avoid routes, locations, and areas with these ships. Maybe in a previous life I was on the Titanic or some other disastrous water voyage. No matter the reason, this phobia prevents me from experiencing aquatic hotels that offer all-you-can eat buffets, constant entertainment, and exquisite travel destinations.

Despite floating in the current of anxiety with cruise ships, I feel I have a decent grip on fear. My personality type allows me to prevent fear from dictating my choices or holding me back from life. I take risks: some calculated, like not having children; some physical, like zip lining in the Dominican Republic or living by myself abroad; others professional, like not settling at a company for comfort; and some personal, like supporting Jim's path to rebuild himself. These are just some examples of how I define risks in my journey.

Meanwhile, it is important to point out that when people ask me if fear is a reason for not having a child, some of them are asking based on what they have experienced. From the capability to be a good

---

4   Louise Delagran, MA, MEd, "Impact of Fear and Anxiety," *Taking Charge of Your Health and Wellbeing*, University of Minnesota, 2021, https://www.takingcharge.csh.umn.edu/impact-fear-and-anxiety.

5   Northwestern Medicine, "5 Things You Never Knew About Fear," October 2020, https://www.nm.org/healthbeat/healthy-tips/emotional-health/5-things-you-never-knew-about-fear.

parent to the fear of losing one's identity to even society's influence, fear is a constant element that no parenting class, book, or group can completely erase. Based on discussions I've had, I understand how fear could be a legitimate reason to not have a child. In my case, it truly wasn't a driver, but for others, it was.

Many women have explained to me their fear of pregnancy and childbirth. Some are so afraid that it created an unstable environment and negatively overpowered the miraculous journey.

My manager at work was deathly afraid of the epidural and the pain childbirth could cause. This fear consumed her to the point of physical sickness and intense anxiety. She told her coworkers that the fear she had with each baby milestone—first kick, detailed sonograms, and healthy growth results—prevented her from experiencing the pure bliss most parents experience during these moments. After the nine months of self-inflicted torture, she finally gave birth and realized the anticipation was worse than the pain itself.

A friend's aunt significantly questioned her capability to be a mom. She was never around children and did not view herself as the "motherly" type. This anxiety allowed her mind to develop negative scenarios which amplified the fear and doubt. My friend detailed how her aunt joined every support group, took CPR and child safety classes, read as many books as possible, and took multiple birthing and nurturing classes. Though these actions seem responsible, her fear caused trust issues. Each class attended or doctor visited was cause for a new registration to confirm the information. It got to a point where genuine advice became too confusing for the aunt, and she started to doubt others as well. Feeling alone and lost, she developed high blood pressure due to the stress. Needing to have an emergency caesarean due to her self-inflicted worry, her instincts kicked in, and all doubt went to the wayside once that baby was born.

With these instances, both women stated that fear itself was worse than the overall outcome, and this realization allowed for a better understanding of what they should expect when expecting.

Regarding other mothers, the fear of pain didn't exist. Though I can't help but think the stitches in your hoo-ha or your caesarean did not tickle, you literally birthed a human. Everyone should give you permission to be afraid or state how painful it was.

Parents also have other fears when it comes to children. Societal influence on their child's life is an increasingly growing concern. It's human nature to desire social belonging, and the parents I have spoken to recognize the significance society has through social media, community, and news. Children today are much more exposed and susceptible to external influences, which create parallel worlds parents either don't agree with or are not aware of. The fear of fighting society's perspective versus the parent's reality is becoming all too common. Worrying about negative persuasion, heading down the wrong path, enforcing ideals that are not realistic, engaging with inappropriate people, or placing impractical expectations on oneself are examples in which parents believe society will speak louder than themselves. Approaching the topic is complicated, and most parents will continuously look for the parenting balance between restriction, acceptance, understanding, and guidance, all while learning to adapt and fight society's charisma and power.

People who know my family understand life is centralized around autism. I have two sisters who each have an adult autistic son. It isn't a secret that these two families struggle. Imagine not being able to understand what your child needs at the age of eighteen or getting beat up every time you say no to your child's wants? Take a moment to think about the life you envisioned for your child, only to take another moment to realize that life will never happen.

With a non-special needs child, your attention goes to that person. With a special needs child, it's not just your attention; it's your entire life. The hardest obstacle for our family was getting over the image of what a childhood *should* be. No little league, no fishing with Grandpa, no baking with Grandma, no milestone moments. Though heartbreaking as this realization was, it does not affect Max or Ryan the same way.

The fears of a parent with a special needs child are as unique and complex as the child themselves. Still, there are common fears within the community: Are we doing enough? Will their communication skills develop? What sort of future will they have? Will I have to choose to let them go, and what will happen after I die? You are striving to find that balance between supporting your special needs child and allowing them to be independent, with the constant fear that society might shame, services won't be provided, meltdowns will occur, or the child may unintentionally hurt themselves. An everyday chore such as grocery shopping could turn into the cops being called because the child had a meltdown in the store. With one flipped cart and a screaming child biting themselves, police are called because outsiders view the situation as destructive or fear they are in danger. Meanwhile, this poor soul is acting out because the lights were too bright, and they were out of nacho cheese Doritos.

You want to bring your kid into the world but fear what the day could bring. Sometimes the world isn't ready to experience your child and vice versa. Max and Ryan, for the most part, will always be dependent on someone, and the truth is, no one knows them better than their parents. We all have an undeniable fear regarding the boys' future, but as a family, we can prepare together and simply provide Max and Ryan the love and life they deserve each day.

When people are aware of my nephews, they wonder if I feared my child would be autistic as well. The answer is both yes and no. When I decided not to have children at the age of sixteen, Max and Ryan were not born yet. Though I have watched my nephews grow up to become great individuals, I've also watched my sisters and brothers-in-law, Phillip and Michael, suffer. Yes, raising a child in general is difficult, but I can't emphasize the extreme extent families who have children with disabilities experience. Since the odds are high, one hundred percent I would be afraid my child would be autistic. Please keep in mind that I am not saying being autistic is a bad attribute or a reason to not have a child. I am simply calling myself selfish this one time. Seeing my sisters and the autistic community raise children is just too emotional for me. From a completely different viewpoint, what happens if I did have a child, and they were not autistic? How would that impact the family? I know the child would be embraced and loved, but I believe there would be a significant amount of warranted questioning, sadness, and jealousy.

All in all, Jim and I know my family will need help—financially, physically, and mentally. If I were to have a child now, I need to think long-term. There is a possibility it could be Jim, my child, and my adult nephews if circumstances happened. Though this is not the main reason I decided not to have children, it does impact it. For Max and Ryan, they come first, and if that means supporting only them in the future, this fun aunt and uncle will gladly take on that double duty.

Richard Bach's fable, *Jonathan Livingston Seagull*, is the story of a seagull who, frustrated with meaningless conformities, soars past his pack and capitalizes on new challenges and adventures. His passion and curiosity ostracize him from his societal flock, but in the end he understands independence and passion as being more important.[6]

Through his flight path and story, one can recognize the necessity and freedom to be yourself, not allowing fear, society, or expectations to stand in your way. With the little time devoted to your life, it is important to remember you can't control the wind, but you can adjust the sail.

---

6   Richard Bach, *Jonathan Livingston Seagull*, (New York: Macmillan Publishers, 1970).

Chapter 8
PASSPORT STAMPS

"Family is everything."

The world is built on so many wonders, and I have been fortunate enough to experience some of them. I have met wonderful people, participated in key cultural rituals, eaten incredible food, and visited amazing environments. With that, I also witnessed extreme divisiveness, poverty, and contrasting ways of living. Those experiences not only humbled me but made me more grateful for my life and the world we live in.

Throughout my travels, I've learned there are words universally understood without even speaking. Love can be shown through a comforting embrace or a sincere smile. Sadness is represented by true tears of pain. Anger proves that the resting bitch face is a global phenomenon.

During my journeys, I was able to view the different meanings of materialistic avenues as well. Being rich in the US has a completely different meaning than being rich in a small town such as, Bauru, Brazil. For the United States, richness is associated with monetary value, celebrity lifestyles, and materialistic objects, assuming that the wealthier you are, the easier your life must be, while being rich in Bauru is based on the importance of your surroundings and the people in your life. Though they understand the necessity money brings, the value of that currency does not compare to the value of family and honor.

Priorities are pivoting in life, and the ideal lifestyle is expanding. Though still a societal abnormality to not have children, it is a decision becoming more popular for many reasons.

An article from Today.com highlighted the title story: "Child-free by choice: Why many women are intentionally opting out of parenthood." In the article, author Kait Hanson details Rachel Cargle's decision to not have children with an emphasis that this decision is not a lonely one.[1]

Cargle, who is an author and activist, established The Loveland Foundation in 2018 to help give Black women and girls access to therapy and mental health resources. Through an interview, the article detailed Rachel's explanation that not having kids was not her intention. Instead, she had the intent to check all of life's boxes: job, marriage, and kids. Motherhood was a requisite of her womanhood, and the desire was on basic auto pilot.

Rachel worked the majority of her adult life as a nanny, which provided a vision into experiencing parenthood. With this immersive view, she was able to fully understand what she loved about the experience of parenthood. Viewing the overall materialistic aspect of it outweighed the extensive parts of being a parent. Having a tight understanding of this reaction, her preconceived notion of being a mom diminished.

Highlighting key concerns society throws at people who decide to not have children, Rachel communicates that this culturally constructed path is a bumpy trip—especially due to those indicating key worries such as avoiding natural paths of life, missing out on something bigger than themselves, and not being fulfilled.

---

1   Kait Hanson, "Child-free by choice: Why many women are intentionally opting out of parenthood," *Today*, March 2, 2021, https://www.today.com/parents/child-free-choice-why-women-intentionally-opt-out-parenthood-t210203.

Sound familiar?

Also detailed in the article was Rachel's explanation of the honest observations, communication, and introspection it took to make the child-free decision and the courage to vocalize it.

The same article told the story of a husband and wife who, as a team, decided to not have children. They detailed the upfront communication and discussions they had highlighting all the recognitions and consequences they could possibly face by deciding not to have children. In the end, their mutual decision was that their trade-offs and priorities were aligned, and within the big picture, both husband and wife were enough.

From 2018, a larger trend indicates the number of babies born in the US fell to the lowest level in thirty-two years with a continuous decline. Voluntary childless statistics show many uptick trends. In 2018, 20 percent of women between the ages of thirty-five and thirty-nine are childless with 15 percent being childless between the ages of forty-five and fifty.[2] Compare that to the 15 percent for ages thirty-five to thirty-nine and 10 percent for ages forty-five and fifty back in 2010.[3] Statistics show in 2021, 57 percent of American couples are childless, compared to roughly 29 percent back in 2012.[4]

Even though statistics within this nature can be influenced with other factors to consider, when multiple channels state the same information, the increased direction of a voluntary childless life is hard to debate.

From my global experiences, I found acceptance of my child-free

2   Erin Duffin, "Percentage of childless women in the United States in 2018, by ethnic group," *Statista*, October 5, 2002, https://www.statista.com/statistics/241538/percentage-of-childless-women-in-the-us-by-ethnic-group/.

3   Neil Shah, "More U.S. Women Are Going Childless," *Wall Street Journal*, April 7, 2015, https://www.wsj.com/articles/BL-REB-31774.

4   US Census Bureau, "First-Ever Census Bureau Report Highlights Growing Childless Older Adult Population," August 31, 2021, https://www.census.gov/newsroom/press-releases/2021/childless-older-adult-population.html#:~:text=Highlights%20include%3A,were%20more%20educated%20than%20parents.

choice interesting. Not once did I feel judged, dismissed, or pitied for not having children. I was not told that my life was insignificant or wrong because I wasn't following a set of values or social norms. Maybe this was due to the language barrier or messages lost in translation, but I don't believe that was the case. Just like being able to detect common emotions in any language, people's sincerity and interest was genuine and detectable.

It's fair to state I was limited in my exposures, so I do understand I am characterizing moments universally. With that said, every race, religion, and culture wanted to hear my story, while wishing me happiness. I am sure some did not agree with my choice and simply internalized the opposition. That is fortunate for me, since *"Du wirst deine Entscheidung bereuen!"* sounds pretty extreme in German versus the American counterpart: "You'll regret your decision!"

As you might have gathered, some conversations in the United States have been opinionated, judgmental, critical, argumentative, invasive, and close-minded. You hear stereotypes of Americans being righteous, entitled, or rude, and some of my conversations reflected that: People who are ready to tell you why you are wrong but not listening to your reasoning, or judging everything and everyone based on biased information, viewpoints, and ignorance.

Hell, sometimes I think that I can inadvertently fall into one or two of those attributes occasionally. I am an East Coast woman at heart. I walk and talk fast, demonstrate impatience, swear (obviously), unapologetically live life through my authentic code, and can sometimes draw quick reactions and a temper. With that, I do understand the necessity to balance. I try to be as considerate to others as possible, listen to their views, understand their perspective, and adapt when necessary.

The United States is a large country with vastly different cultures, expectations, and ideologies—a magnificent melting pot of opportunities. With no children and living on the East Coast, I can say the majority of the reactions are the same. No one cares. They are too busy with their children, their jobs, or their financial woes that they don't even blink an eye when I mention that I don't have a child. For the most part, it's common to see married couples in the metropolitan area simply not having kids and focusing on themselves.

Meanwhile in the Midwest, the direct definition between happiness is linked to family and children. On the West Coast, the chill vibe is dominant, allowing you to pursue whatever makes you the happiest. While in the South, it is a combination of all regions. Only in America am I applauded for my independent child-free decision and then challenged for it when traveling to a different US region.

While continuing our travels west, let's go to our neighbors up north, eh? Canada is a large country as well. Full disclosure, I have only been exposed to Toronto and Quebec. From my experiences, Canadians are extremely friendly people.

Canada reminds me of the United States with its diverse group of cultures and religions, large corporations, and manufacturing sites, majestic scenery, and terrains. However, they are obsessed with Tim Hortons coffee (which I just can't wrap my head around).

I'll take my Dunkin to go, please.

Despite the coffee catastrophe, Canada was my second home for a while. I was there every other week for work, and I met some great people. Because I was there so often, everyone joked that I should pursue dual citizenship. Since I was in my twenties at the time, two citizenships were not on my mind, nor were children. When discussing my child-free decision, the Canadians' friendly feedback highlighted the importance to do what is best for me but emphasized that once a life door closes, it sometimes can be difficult or even impossible to reopen.

The line operators were the same each time I went up north. I knew their family and hobbies while they knew a great deal about me. One technician, George, was an older gentleman who opened up about his marriage. He and his wife didn't have children. They wanted children, but after years of trying, they were not able to conceive. George believed the decision was made for him and his wife, and that life's door had shut on their opportunity. Just when George and his wife started accepting their lifestyle, someone came knocking at their closed door. A while back, they had decided to apply for adoption, but the process was tedious and a long shot. They barely made the minimum criteria for consideration, so they believed this option was just a dream. But it happened. They were considered, reviewed, interviewed, and were granted a beautiful baby girl. George knew deep down something was missing in his life before that baby. He also acknowledged the strength of his belief. His feeling for needing a child was just as prominent as my feeling for not wanting one. He understood that power, and though different, he respected it. George never asked me again about children nor reminded me about that infamous door being shut. Clearly there are times it can be open. Instead, our conversations were around fatherhood and baby Clara.

The Canadians I met supported whatever decision I made, but they reminded me to remain open-minded. To this day, I love their well-disposed demeanor and their ketchup. Yes, their ketchup is straight up better than the United States'.

While North America is fabulous, let's jet set to some other continents I have been to. I spent a fair amount of time in South America, but only in the countries of Colombia and Brazil. The city of Cali in Colombia was beautiful. So vibrant and picturesque, and to this day some of the best fruit I have ever had in my life. The people are extremely adventurous, proud of their country, and center themselves around family. I learned more about my coworkers' families in one week than I know about some of my US friends' families. Every coworker had, wanted, or was trying for children. Not having a child wasn't a consideration. However, if someone like me stated they didn't want children, their response did not indicate my choice was wrong. Instead, they graciously reminded me that if God's plan revolved around children, He would provide me guidance and opportunity. There was no debate, just a simple consideration. It is clear for Colombians that the growth of family and religion is extremely important, and though not having children can happen, it was rare with the families I spoke with.

I spent six months in Brazil starting up a new production facility site. I spent the majority of that time in Bauru, which is about three and a half hours west of Sao Paulo. Bauru is a small, industrial town with local restaurants and familiar corner gatherings. Just like Cali, they were some of the nicest and family-centric people I have ever met. Generations are so instrumental in life, along with traditions and culture. Pride for their country parallels the pride they have for their family.

Four generations of the same family were at a small local fish restaurant I went to, sitting at a small, cramped table, sipping beer and eating the catch of the day. I asked the owner if they had any ties to the restaurant. He simply stated the grandfather had been going there since he worked at the welding plant across the street. That is amazing. To this day, the only place I continue to go to is my parent's house.

With my discussions of children, my experience in Bauru had similarities to Colombia. Family is everything, and children are the key to the future. What I also experienced was that being an aunt or uncle who instills knowledge, morals, and love was sufficient in life as well. Of course, a child of your own is the ultimate blessing, but the love provided to others is just as powerful. For me, Brazil's response assured my responsibility to be an amazing role model for my nephews. They also showed the importance of growing a family tree, but without the root, there would be no tree to grow.

Continuing my journey, I spent a large amount of time in both China and Thailand, beautiful areas that are rich in history, cuisine, and culture. In Thailand, I spent most of my time in the industrial area about an hour west of Bangkok. The people I met did not feel comfortable with the English language, so we mostly got by with gestures and a commonality of our business. I was there developing and manufacturing a new innovative confectionery product, and I spent the majority of my time at the plant, sometimes for twenty-four hours straight. But again, a smile, a concerned eyebrow raise, a thumbs up, or even a stern look of disappointment is universal. So we got by.

When I did have a chance to go back to my hotel in Bangkok, there were more tourists and people who spoke English. I remember asking the concierge for a map and then taking the train on my own to certain stops. I was in the center of the city where I would go to the local restaurants, the malls, and grocery stores.

The first time I went, my coworkers and I did touristy things like go to the Royal Palace, ride around in tuk tuks, go to the outdoor markets, and eat at places where English was anticipated. The two other times I went, I witnessed more of the city on my own to explore its depth. That is where I met some great people. Instead of always eating the hotel breakfast, I went down the street to a Thai bakery and ordered something different each time. I had no idea what items I bought, but I wanted to go beyond the standard tourist flavors.

What stood out were the local family businesses and the children running around, doing their homework and helping in the store. There were no babysitters or technology. Just kids sitting in the corner coloring, sweeping, or chasing one another.

I went to this man who had a stand on the corner by my hotel. He sold green nuts dusted in chili powder. They were extremely inexpensive, and he had his child with him supporting the business. I went every single day and ordered a bag for the ride to work. Rain or shine, he would always have my bag ready for me. When my production and start-up was complete, I knew I was taking my last ride to the site, so the concierge helped me write a note in Thai explaining that I was leaving and expressing my appreciation for him and his child. I went up to the cart and handed him an envelope, while he handed me my delicious treat. In the envelope, I left him three thousand baht, which at the time equaled one hundred US dollars. Keep in mind my bag of nuts cost thirty baht.

When I returned from work later that night, the concierge handed me a note. It was from Jule, the man's seven-year-old son, who thanked me for my kindness and worldly generosity. Even though I never had a full conversation regarding children from my multiple trips to Thailand, I did witness that family, respect, and hard work are core values.

While on the east end of the world, I continued my travels to China. I have had the pleasure of visiting both Beijing and Guangzhou, two radically different areas, one being the epicenter of everything and the other being extremely industrial. Though different in their positioning, they were similar in personality with extremely diligent, introverted, process-following, extraordinary people. Conversations were very brief and to the point. Emotional attachment or initiation of conversations did not really exist, but intrigue and connection did.

A local coworker set up a dinner for me and his family at an authentic hot pot restaurant while in Beijing. His wife and friends spoke decent English, so we were able to communicate with less barriers. Food was plentiful, adult beverages were flowing, and the conversation was staccato yet engaging.

At first the family and friends were surprised I was willing to try anything local. Their experiences with Americans involved steak, beer, potatoes, and bread. So when I asked for the tripe, different seafoods, and Chinese greens, they were proudly impressed, which drove conversations. Not overly boisterous or loud, everyone at the table had small smiles and happy expressions while discussing topics.

"Do you like all kinds of food?" one person asked.

"Actually, no. I don't like red meat, cheese, or sauces. And I am not a huge fan of chocolate. But I will try something local out of respect and wonder," I said.

Normally, in the US, if someone hears I dislike American food staples, I end up being on trial. But with this group, we sat there in brief silence afterwards until another person brought up another topic.

"Do you like working as a product scientist?" another person asked.

"Yes. I feel comfortable with this career and enjoy what I do. What do you all do?" I asked in return.

"Finance."

"Teacher."

"New mom."

"Congratulations!" I enthusiastically stated to the new mom at the table.

With a small smile, she replied, "Thank you."

"Are you glad to be out of the house?" I asked.

Staring directly into my eyes, she took a deep breath and said, "Yes!"

"Do you have children?" she asked.

"No, I decided I did not want to have children. It's just me and my husband," I answered.

And with a small nod of sincerity and approval, the woman said, "That's enough."

After that, our conversations focused on work, but overall, our small talk was both direct and seemingly profound.

Every person I met in China showed me respect and had a secure guard up. It wasn't until they felt comfortable with me that those guards were dropped, their confidence grew, and their emotions showed.

I decided to do some touristy things in Beijing. I walked the Great Wall of China, I went to their tech malls, and I traveled to their history and political museums. I also explored on my own. Hopping on a trolly and following a large crowd to a dumpling shop where no one spoke English, I somehow managed to get by, probably because that large crowd made room for the only American within a twenty-five-mile radius to sit. I pointed to some items on the menu, ate what the locals ordered—which by the way was just spectacular—and was given a lesson on different chopstick abilities!

Besides recovering from my noodle and dumpling coma, I was able to experience other culture ideologies. Family, from what I gathered, is important, but it is about quality vs. quantity. China does have significant overpopulation, so for the most part I sensed old school tradition. Children are an extraordinary gift. A boy being welcomed first into the family is a virtue, and typically one or two children is the limit.

I also got the impression that with or without children, success is measured through your career. Based on the hustle and continuous work principles I witnessed, emphasis isn't only focused on building a family but also on stable success. Don't get me wrong; success can be defined as a happy family, but that family must be provided for.

When I was discussing not wanting a child, no one thought twice about it. Instead, the real interest occurred when they realized I had married a Chinese man. All of sudden, their English stopped, and Mandarin started.

WHOA . . . Go back to English, please!

I understand I've been with my husband and his family for an exceptionally long time, but Mandarin is a difficult language. If the topics don't revolve around "How are you?", counting to ten, "I love you," "I don't know," and "Thank you," then this conversation could end badly. Once they realized I couldn't speak their language, their honest feedback for not having kids was simply that they understood. Those two words are so basic, yet powerfully accepting and reassuring.

The last stop on my continental tour holds a special place in my heart. I was lucky enough to live in South Africa for a short-term assignment. I stayed in Johannesburg and traveled to Botswana, Egypt, The Kingdom of Swaziland, Port Elizabeth, Pretoria, and Cape Town. During this time, I met incredible people and made real connections and memories that will last a lifetime—memories such as when South Africans experienced their first snowstorm in over twenty years. They were petrified but excited!

While Johannesburg, Pretoria, Port Elizabeth, and Cape Town all had similar vibes and features, Botswana and Swaziland had their own. The true nature of Afrikaans highlights the importance of family. I experienced that through numerous *braais* I was invited to. Imagine an American barbecue with more food, more liquor, and more family members. That is my general description of a braai: an all-day event with every single family member and friend you could think of focusing on good conversations, love, and thankfulness.

Humbleness and appreciation for what they have is abundant, and children are opportunities for family life to support positive changes in the South African culture. Children are looked upon to instill history and knowledge, to mold a better society, and to continue values and family traditions. They follow in the footsteps of Nelson Mandela and continuously advance from the apartheid; however, having a child, in my opinion, is not a basis of existence for people in these areas. Progressing their lives for a better and stable environment is key, and if a child fits that definition, then so be it.

South Africans in the lower states wondered if I would ever change my mind about children, and of course, the answer I always provided was no. That response encouraged them to emphasize the importance of family. One interesting fact about my South African living experience was that it brought me a second family. Since I was so far away from my blood relatives and friends, key people took me in and treated me like their own, right off the bat—another example indicating how important the definition of family is.

Areas such as The Kingdom of Swaziland and Botswana did not have signs of large city life but more of a rural industrial side. I saw families with a lot more kids and unity of community. A fulfilled life must include children, a strong work ethic, and devoted religion. Talking to the locals about having kids got more of an expressive reaction versus a verbal one. The locals automatically assumed I had children and wondered where they were while I was living in South Africa. Once I told them I did not have kids, their expressions changed to a wide-eyed, tall posture. I assumed they were shocked, though I fully don't know their thoughts since the topic ended after those encounters.

On my final journey, I traveled to Egypt. My discussions about my personal life were extremely limited, and I was minimally exposed to family lifestyle. With the small interactions I had, it was obvious that family—children, parents, grandparents, siblings, aunts, uncles, etc.—are the identity of their well-being, and protecting the family is the number one priority. Where I stayed in Cairo and Alexandria, pride and protection run deep, especially the importance and need for children to carry on family values, traditions, legacy, and pride.

I fully believe that we travel not to escape life but for life not to escape us. In many cases, exposure to different cultures, religions, history, and even food can broaden one's perspective of the world and even oneself. My global journey has proven to expand my acceptance and independence, all while emphasizing the importance of children. One thing universally holds true: family can be defined in many ways, with the common denominator always being the need to feel like we're home.

Chapter 9
THE LAST TRIMESTER

"Success and fulfillment come in all forms, from CEO to KIDS or even both!"

The decision to have children is a choice as unique as the person making it. Unfortunately, too many people feel at liberty to impose their beliefs onto others. It is important to base your life decisions on your own values and morals, especially something as personal as having children. Those moments are too intimate, and a dictated expectation might not fit your reality.

Remember that.

Remember who you are, what you're made of, and why you live the life you do. I encourage you to listen but be strong enough to politely disagree when necessary. The same determination and passion you have for your beliefs is mirrored by those explaining theirs. The odds are low that you'll change your view over a quick conversation, but respect should be just as common as how you define fulfillment.

As simple as this sounds, it is a complicated and delicate act. We live in a world that is continuously evolving. People become more expressive, expose themselves to key convictions, and verbalize their thoughts with different forms of communication. Emotions grow high, combativeness sometimes turns to dismissiveness, and defensive behavior surfaces. It is inevitable, but we all need to remain grounded and remember the true fundamentals of humanity.

I find myself practicing basic habits when discussing my child-free decision. Most importantly, since respect is something I anticipate from others, I must provide it. I make it a point to give the person my full attention. That way I can listen, comprehend better, and think before I act. One must ensure they understand the person's point of view before discussing. This can be a difficult step since emotions sometimes overcome rationality—especially when you feel like you are on trial.

I mentioned in the beginning the Hot Mess Express, and honestly it does make some unwanted stops. It is difficult—sometimes damn right impossible—to not take comments directed at one's beliefs or choices personally. The most important aspect to remember in those situations is to breathe in order to calm your tone, pulse, and mind. The exact situation someone is throwing at you is not the way you need to counteract. Be the bigger person by fighting fire with a fire extinguisher, not fire with fire. You also will need to remember there are two people in the conversation. Put yourself in their shoes. It is important to fully understand where they are coming from and why. Ask questions, engage in the conversation, be open, and simulate walking a mile in said shoes. Though I know it might feel like all you do is walk in others' shoes, it should be stated that this must apply to both parties.

The decision not to have a child is a difficult one. The mental seesaw someone goes through when contemplating this choice is extremely complicated. Even though it might seem effortless from my journey to make this decision, I must emphasize that pressure and discussions weigh heavy on the mind. You can be the most independent and confident person, but with a judging and influential world surrounding you, even the most assured person reflects a mirror with two faces. There are constant reminders of accepted societal norms that stare directly at you while you purposefully stare back defying them. Your character is being tested and always on full display. When it comes to a child-free decision, you must mentally battle the questions cultivated for your life choice and determine your daily approach:

Must I be on defense all the time?

Do I have to explain myself every time?

Will this judgement last my whole life?

What did I give up?

Am I enough?

I have been on my journey for quite some time, and without an ounce of doubt I can say it is a work in progress. I need to constantly remind myself to practice what I preach and to not lose sight of who I am. I've had many conversations with people who barely know me. It is my responsibility to explain what defines me, be more personable, and give insight into my life. This is the best way for people to see my perspective, understand who Danielle really is, and allow the conversation to feel welcomed. One should not be afraid to announce strengths and use that same platform to grow from flaws.

Conversations are meant to be opportunities for expressiveness. Curiosity, knowledge, and passion all persuade interaction and the drive of a discussion. For everyone involved, tone, facial expressions, and even understanding boundaries are quite important in establishing context. I try to respond in a manner that supports my point of view. Sometimes that means adapting to the direction the conversation is going, while other times it is understanding when to walk away. This is yet another example of something I must continuously practice: when to know the discussion is mute and ties should be cut. It is extremely difficult walking away, knowing your point was not heard and their perception of you is askew. When it is necessary to walk away, I remind myself about numbers. I might not have convinced one person who I am, but that one person should not dictate my life. That role is already filled by me.

Each day will provide an experience, and as long as you remember who you are and what your life is about, other factors will fall into place. For me, my life consists of living some distance from my family. I make it a point to speak to my mom every day and visit as often as I can. I will never miss the opportunity to go home for Christmas. Family, nostalgia, and my mom's Christmas menu all bring me to my home in Dover, New Jersey. I make it a point to get there a few days before Christmas to visit with friends. The majority of the time Jim comes with me, and because our time is limited, we plan accordingly. We schedule dinner trips to kid-friendly restaurants for our friends who have children, knowing the majority of the dinner a child will be on my lap, a newborn might throw up on me, or I will be playing with a toddler. I wouldn't have it any other way. I also feel that no matter the distance or time that has passed, we instantly pick up right where we left off.

After we hand the kiddos back to their parents, we go to my mom's house to prepare for Christmas Eve and Day. I help my mom cook, straighten up the house, and run any additional errands that she might need. Christmas festivities come, and my immediate family is there. Max walks in the door and automatically asks me to tickle his back. Aunt Danielle sits with Max on the couch for hours, simply tickling his back while he listens to "Rudolph" on his iPad. Ryan comes in, and I get a giant hug and an "I love you" in a sweet voice. He sits on the other side of the couch, and Danielle is in a nephew sandwich. Again, I wouldn't want it any other way. When I am able to move from the couch, I make sure to wrap as many gifts as possible for Max, who loves to open presents. There isn't a large amount of excitement around the presents themselves, just the act of opening gifts. If he is having a particularly hard time, everyday items in the house will get gift wrapped so he can feel calm and happy. The same goes for Ryan. I will support my sisters and brothers-in-law in any way I can, because that's what family does.

After the holiday happiness, it is back to reality, where my day is jammed packed with responsibilities: working forty-plus hours a week, supporting the growth of the company I work for and my direct reports, answering the whiny meows of my cat Taj, and planning my next challenge or adventure with my husband.

Jim is at the dinner table finishing up his homework and finalizing his MBA platform. I am sitting on the couch looking through our bills, researching when to participate in the next autism awareness event, catching up on text messages, exercising on the treadmill while watching reality TV, and realizing it is time for a group trip.

Sometimes the best feeling in life is normalcy—like settling into your routine at home. Just imagine how comfortable you are with a mattress that is specifically designed to your needs for a relaxing sleep. The set temperature in your house is balanced for both your physical and mental state, or the flame is the perfect height to get an even pan sear for a delicious dinner. All those items become mundane and a part of your life.

Now imagine how you feel the first time you are in a new place. The mattress has a weird concave in the center. The temperature in the house is too hot for you to function, and the stove is electric. You never assume those minor adjustments could cause such a shift, but they do. The same goes for choices made in society. When going against the expected, basic normalities that are accepted tend to be that lumpy mattress. It can take a while to get used to, and in some circumstances, you never do. But what people forget is that you don't need to keep that lumpy mattress. If you don't like it, fine, you can move on to a Sleep Number and create your own personal setting.

Our culture has accepted two huge lies: If you disagree with someone's belief or lifestyle, then you must fear or hate them; and to like or love someone, you need to fully agree with their beliefs. It simply can't be that black and white. In today's world, people should not know the price of everything but the value of nothing.

I am extremely appreciative and fortunate for the gift of life, my ability to choose for myself, and pure authenticity. Humbly I applaud myself for the courageous decision to not have a child. For those of you like me, give yourself a round of applause as well. Those who have children, I am providing you all a standing ovation! You see, it is not a woman's duty to give birth, but it can be their calling or desire. A person can be established with or without a child because success comes in all forms.

From CEO to KIDS or even both, society does have two faces: the one that stares at you from afar and the one that is directly from your own perspective. Be the louder voice to advocate for your beliefs. Enjoy the life that has been given to you, and by all means, raise a glass, toast to your awesomeness, and get milk drunk.